"Seldom is it the case
and godly compass
Authentic Power by J
one godly man can
cogently and compassionately in a single volume."

–PAIGE PATTERSON

President, Southwestern Baptist Theological Seminary

Fort Worth, Texas

"My good friend John Avant has written a practical prophetic book—prophetic in the sense that it's the right message at the right time. Followers of Christ so desperately need a fresh understanding and experience of the resurrection power of our Savior. Thank you, John, for calling us back to the essence of effective Christianity!"

–DR. CRAWFORD W. LORITTS JR.

Author/speaker

Senior Pastor, Fellowship Bible Church, Roswell, GA

"John Avant's *Authentic Power* reminds us that the greatest energy crisis in America is the result of the underutilized human soul, originally designed to run on high-octane, Holy Spirit–inspired power. *Authentic Power* teaches us to not just cope but triumph over life's challenges."

–DAN CATHY

Owner/president, Chick-fil-A

"Most people only experience life in one dimension. *Authentic Power* opens the door to the world we don't see with our eyes and don't fight by human strength. Avant helps readers understand the incredible power available to all who are in Christ. It's a power promise you can't afford to pass by."

–BOB RECCORD

President, North American Mission Board

AUTHENTIC
POWER

JOHN AVANT

Multnomah® Publishers *Sisters, Oregon*

AUTHENTIC POWER
published by Multnomah Publishers, Inc.
© 2006 by John Avant

International Standard Book Number: 1-59052-469-1

Cover design by Kirk DouPonce, DogEaredDesign.com
Cover image by PixelWorks Studios, www.shootPW.com
Interior design and typeset by Katherine Lloyd, The DESK

Italics in Scripture are the author's emphasis.
Unless otherwise indicated, Scripture quotations are from:
The Holy Bible, New International Version
© 1973, 1984 by International Bible Society,
used by permission of Zondervan Publishing House

Other Scripture quotations are from:
The Holy Bible, King James Version (KJV)

Multnomah is a trademark of Multnomah Publishers, Inc.,
and is registered in the U.S. Patent and Trademark Office.
The colophon is a trademark of Multnomah Publishers, Inc.

Printed in the United States of America

For information:
MULTNOMAH PUBLISHERS, INC.
601 N LARCH STREET • SISTERS, OREGON 97759

Library of Congress Cataloging-in-Publication Data

Avant, John, 1960-
Authentic power / by John Avant.
     p. cm.
Includes bibliographical references.
ISBN 1-59052-469-1
1. Resurrection. 2. Power (Christian theology) I. Title.
BT482.A93 2006
269--dc22   2005026119

06 07 08 09 10—10 9 8 7 6 5 4 3 2 1 0

To all of my friends in the persecuted church
and to the courageous missionaries
who come beside them.

You are the most powerful people I know.

CONTENTS

ACKNOWLEDGMENTS

To my incredible family:
Mom, Dad, Michael, Cindy, and all of yours—
thanks for the life we share.

To my wife, Donna—this is fun!
Let's do twenty-five more.

To my children: Christi, Amy, and Trey.
You are my greatest adventure.

Thanks to my assistant Meg, who for almost
a decade has kept me sane. You are family.

Thanks to my great friends Doug Munton, Dave Buck,
and Rosemary Preston for reading, proofing, and advising.

Thanks to my new family at the North American
Mission Board. Wow! We get to do this for a living.

I love Indian food. Just a few months ago, after years of mouthwatering waiting, the first Indian restaurant opened in our town. I could hardly wait for that first bite of flaming, curried goodness. My friend Gary was my lucky lunch partner for that meal. We had shared some wonderfully deep spiritual conversations over the years, but on this day he was quieter than usual. That meant that nothing much was being said, since my mouth was stuffed with chicken vindaloo.

Suddenly, in a voice edged with conviction and bordering on frustration, Gary blurted out, "Where is the power that raised Jesus from the dead, John? Where is it?" Now, it took a lot to make me pause, fork in midair, and delay my next bite long enough to figure out what he was talking about, but he had my attention.

"I'm confused," he said. "I'm happy that we're all discovering our purpose. That's really important. I believe in worship and fellowship, discipleship, evangelism, all that. But there has to be more! It's supposed to be supernatural—following Jesus. Where is the power the New

Testament church had? Where's the power of the resurrection?"

Wow! Gary had no idea that the same question he was asking right then had been burning in my own heart as intensely as the spices in my mouth. Our church had just finished the 40 Days of Purpose campaign, and it was incredible. My friend Rick Warren's book *The Purpose Driven Life* had given our church a clear focus, just as it has for thousands of other churches. Our church was large, healthy, and growing. What more could I ask for?

Authentic power. That's what I was asking for! Power to fill the purposes of our lives and our church. Power to ensure that worship, fellowship, discipleship, ministry, and evangelism didn't just become "the stuff we are supposed to do to be a good church." I wanted the power that ignites the purpose. I wanted purpose on fire!

And if I were completely honest with myself, I didn't often see it. Could I really say that our church resembled the church in the book of Acts? Overflowing with the power of the Spirit and transforming our world? No. Not consistently, at least.

And what about other churches? I have the chance to speak at many, and it seemed to me that virtually all of them faced the same power outage. In fact, many weren't even concerned with the lack of power. They were too busy with the vital issues of daily church life—like whether to clap in worship, why the youth group's music had to be so loud, and when their Sunday school classroom was ever going to get painted—to even notice that the power of God seemed absent.

And if I really wanted to be honest, even among the churches that were growing and baptizing large numbers, few of them were reaching many truly unchurched converts. A staff member of a new church in our area told one of our staff that they had nearly emptied a couple of other churches when they started up. And he seemed to think that was a good thing! Sounds like swapping fish among aquariums more than fishing!

And in my own denomination, as in evangelicalism as a whole, when some really do begin to see the unchurched reached, the reaction from other church leaders is rarely rejoicing. It is usually criticism of contemporary methodology, which may be based more on jealousy than on any legitimate concern.

What's going on? Are we just all out of power? Is it no longer available to us? To our churches? Do we have to choose between business-as-usual church life and wild claims of the supernatural from ego-centered guys on television begging us to send for their anointed prayer cloth for a donation of only a hundred dollars?

Where is *the power of the resurrection?*

Great question, Gary. Maybe *the* question that must be answered for our churches to matter again, for our lives to be fueled by New Testament fire instead of by the dead wood of our own efforts.

I didn't have a full answer for Gary that day, but I do know where it can be found. I've been there. Let me take you there.

A STEP INTO POWER

I stood quietly by myself on a bright, beautiful morning, waiting for the crowd in front of me to clear. *Was* **the** *day as beautiful as this day, Lord?* Finally, I saw the chance I had been waiting for. The last person exited, and no one else was waiting. I could go in for a few minutes on my own.

I stepped into the garden tomb just outside the walls of Jerusalem. I was struck by how small it was. Such a tiny place to change a whole world. I reached out my hand and touched the coolness of the hewn rock. I knelt and touched the place—what may indeed be the very place where the body of Jesus once lay. Overwhelmed, I stood, and then I saw it. The view Jesus had as He stepped out of the tomb. I was frozen—transfixed by the strange thought that I could not step out. I could not take the same step my Lord took— the step that saved me, the step that opened up a new life for me that I did not deserve. I could not step out of the tomb.

But in one moment of utter, life-changing amazement it hit me—I already had! "Having been buried with him in baptism and *raised with him* through your faith in the power of God, who raised him from the dead" (Colossians 2:12). I stepped out of the tomb with Jesus on the day He rose! Even then, I was on His mind. Though it makes no sense, I was His choice. I was raised with Him!

And so I stepped out of the tomb—again. And in that step is found the answer to Gary's question. Here was resurrection power. Walking with Jesus out of the tomb! But what would it mean to live like that? How would it flesh out in the real world? How would it change us and our churches? What do you look like when you come out of the tomb? Well, that's what this book is about: *living in the realm of the resurrection*. A place we might not be used to living in. But it is a place that is meant for us—a place I hope we can go to together.

Authentic power is far from absent in our world today. I have seen it many times—often in the most unexpected places. Places where the realm of darkness does desperate battle with the resurrection realm. Let me take you to one of those places. A place where a variety of very different power seekers saw their lives connect in quite an unlikely way.

ON THE OTHER SIDE OF THE WORLD...

Abdul could taste it now. The power was almost in his hands. For so many months he had dreamed of this day—the day when the arrogance of the Americans would be shattered. His humiliation and rage at the enemy presence in his country had reached a boiling point. For America to have any power in the Middle East, in his homeland, was beyond unacceptable.

For so long he had worked to keep it all under control—so that the plan could be a safely kept secret until the right time. Today was that time. No more need for caution. Today all his wrath could overflow. The vengeance of Allah could be unleashed. It was time for the Americans to feel the fire. Time to strike! Time for power!

ON THE OTHER SIDE OF THE CITY...

Mustafa understood well Abdul's quest for power. For so many years it had been his quest as well. How he had poured himself into the study of the Koran. Surely no one had worked harder to please Allah, to know his mighty power. Mustafa would not settle for the watered-down teaching of so many of the weak Muslims. The compromisers. Pandering to the infidels. No. He would give his life to the defense of the truths taught by the prophet Muhammad.

How many could claim with him to have memorized fully half of the prophet's words? And one day he would have the entire Koran committed to memory. He had the best teachers to guide his understanding. As he read the doctrines of the great leader Osama Bin Laden, he felt the contagious power of his hatred grow. With his booming voice, he was the perfect one to chant the call to prayer at his mosque. "There is no God but Allah, and Muhammad is his prophet!" As his words rang through the streets of his city, people bowed by the thousands, brought to worship by his call—*his* call. What power!

But as Mustafa thought back on those days, he found it amazing that he had once been that person. That person was dead, and with him the shadowy evil he had once called power. Something new burned in him now.

Something stronger than the hate, something he had never before seen but had, in some deep place inside, been searching for all his life. Something had risen in him. It was the love of Jesus. The urge to kill out of hate had been conquered by the One who died out of love—for him.

And now it was time for the prayer call again—for his powerful voice once more to be heard on the streets of the city. His call would not come from the mosque now, but from anywhere God placed him. And his call was a call of truth seldom heard in the Middle East—"There is one God, and Jesus is His Son!" Mustafa knew full well that prison might be his home after people heard his call. He had been there more than once already.

But there would be no stopping him. No prison walls could contain the call. He had found a passion and a power that overwhelmed him with joy. He was born again! With that thought, he began to laugh. It started small but soon rose from his mouth in uncontrolled ecstasy. Others had to know this life, this peace. This power. Still laughing, he arose to the call.

THE AMERICAN

He had been foolish. It wasn't the first time, but it was the first time it had cost him his passport and visa. It wasn't very smart to go to an area of this Middle Eastern city known to be occupied by terrorists, but he had been with friends and it seemed relatively safe. Now his bag had been stolen and, with it, his way out of the country and back home again. How stupid! He knew better. He'd been in thirty countries and had never carried his passport in his bag before. There was nothing to do now but head to the American embassy.

No reason to get too upset. He had learned on trips like this to go with the flow and look for the surprising ways that God would work through the most unexpected and sometimes unpleasant events. He had also learned not to get too worked up over what he had no power to control. After all, with what his purpose was here, there was no hope of accomplishing it in his own power anyway.

He had come here to join the war on terrorism. And though he had deep respect and support for those fighting with conventional weapons, his weapons were different. He had come with a passionate belief that the most powerful force on earth is the conquering love of Jesus Christ—a love that could pierce the darkness of the Middle East, even the hate-filled hearts of the most fanatic Muslims.

Most Americans found that hard to believe, but he knew it to be true. He had seen it in the eyes of his friend Mustafa. He had heard it in his laughter, which filled a room like the contagious joy of heaven itself. Even now he held in his hands the most amazing photographs he had ever seen—a picture of Mustafa as a radical Muslim and a second picture of him after he met Christ. The transformation was impossible to describe. It was what "born again" looked like. He would show these pictures to as many people as he could in America. People had to know this power, to see it.

But for now, he had a purpose in this land so far from home. He had traveled here not as the American with all the answers, swooping in to the rescue, but to support the already-growing army here—the army of God's people, transformed by His love, assaulting the darkness with the light of Christ. He had come to be with them for a little while. To learn, to love, and then to go home to support their battle from overseas. He was after the power of God that could literally change the Middle East. A lost passport was a minor inconvenience in the midst of this war.

So on a beautiful spring day, a little frustrated, but happy to be in the hands of the Head of the army, he walked into the American embassy building.

...Abdul's team was ready. The rockets were in place and all nine men knew their responsibility. Soon media from all over the world would be reporting on their glorious accomplishment. Abdul had watched with uncontrolled glee as the towers fell on 9/11. Even though he saw the devastation only on a television screen, he felt as if he were there. This was his battle too, and now it was his turn. Now he would see the destruction of Americans with his own eyes, by his own hand, and the Americans would watch it on their TVs. No more shame at the power of the enemy. Today, the power was his—and Allah's, of course. And so Abdul turned his attention to the preparations for the rocket attacks—the rockets to be launched into the embassy building of the United States of America.

BACK AT HOME...

At first glance, sixteen-year-old Amy didn't appear very powerful. But power was exactly what she was after. She felt something—something that stirred her, frightened her, and left her with an uneasy feeling that something was very wrong. So Amy did what is available to so many but chosen by so few.

She entered the realm of resurrection power. The realm of unimaginable strength.

A young girl slipped to her knees in her bedroom in Georgia, and the heavens opened. Though she could not see it, demons screamed around her to stop. Angels drew their swords and struck. The same power that rolled a stone away from a tomb was unleashed by a mighty hand. And it all came at the quiet whisper of one teenager: "Jesus, protect my daddy!"

The power of God moved like an unseen wave across the world. All the carefully formed plans of the enemy inexplicably began to unravel. The power of the invisible realm had penetrated the visible. Prayers had been heard. Prayers were being answered. The evil anticipation of Abdul and his cohorts was transformed into the bitter rage of frustration and defeat as government forces suddenly burst in. How had they known? How could this be? And their dream of terrorist victory came to an end. They would not end this day in celebration of American deaths, but in a prison cell. The rockets, ready for their appointed destination, would never be launched. And a cry of rage rose from the realm of spiritual darkness.

On the other side of the city, another cry was beginning. A chant that would be strange to Western ears but a familiar sound in the Middle East. A call in loud, cadenced Arabic. Familiar in sound but not in content. Something was different here.

Mustafa stood on the street, tears of joy streaming down his face, the power of God shining from his countenance, and cried, "For God so loved the world that He gave His only begotten Son, that whosoever should believe in Him would not perish, but have eternal life!" And many of those who heard it knew, as Mustafa had come to know, that they were hearing for the first time the words of truth. The power that Abdul had sought, Mustafa had found! And there was no stopping it now.

AS I SAT IN THE EMBASSY BUILDING that day, I had no idea of the drama that was unfolding. The drama that I was very much a part of. The drama that could have taken my life. I was the foolish American! I didn't find out what had happened until I went back to the hotel room and discovered that it was all over the news, all over the world. But that's the way it is with the power of God. He moves in a resurrection realm, an invisible realm, but with very visible results.

I want to know that realm, and I want you to as well. I want to live in it—in the reality of the power of God. I want to live out what I really believe—that adventures like the one I just described are real—and not uncommon at all. They are going on around us all the time. We're just so trained to live in the visible that we rarely even think about the invisible. And that's really tragic.

I lived that adventure during a visit to a country in the Middle East. I've changed the names, but "Mustafa" really is my friend—one of the only full-time evangelists in the world who once followed the teachings of Bin Laden. Abdul represents the nine terrorists who were arrested that day. And others were killed in battles with government forces while I was there.

But what kind of adventure is it if you don't even know you're in it? God's kind!

It's a resurrection realm adventure. When I'm sitting in a chair in an office in the Middle East, God's power is being unleashed across the world. What if I learned to live in and experience power I cannot see? What if we all did? That's the purpose of this book.

GOING BACK

One of the strangest feelings I've ever had was walking down the streets of that city just a few months ago during another visit. I had just heard that all nine terrorists had been sentenced that day—sentenced to hang. I still don't know their fate with any certainty. But I thought a lot about the power and the sovereignty of God as I walked and prayed. Nine terrorists had tried to kill me and many others. They might soon be dead themselves. Yet here I was, walking through their city, alive and bringing the message they hated to their people.

I don't always understand God's ways. I first came to the Middle East because of the murder of a woman whose husband had become a good friend. She was a missionary and was shot by terrorists. I promised her husband that I would do all I could to help reach the people his wife died loving. On my first trip I knelt on the bloodstained floor where she had died. Why had God spared me and taken her? I don't understand. But I know this: I am here and I want to know His power! I want to know what it is. I want to know how to find it.

A passage of Scripture jumped off the page at me after I understood that God had spared my life that day. I read it while I was still in the Middle East, and it gripped me in the way that only one other passage has in my life. I wrote a book about that one, Ephesians 3:20–21, called *The Passion Promise*. I have to write about this one too. It will not let me go until I do. I hope that's because you need to hear God speak through it as much as I do—that you too are tired of missing most of what happens around you because you live only in the visible.

In this passage, we *meet* power in a way that we rarely think about, much less experience. We also find the road to this power and are confronted with the choice of a lifetime: take it, or meander down the powerless paths of the visible realm until we die—and realize what we missed!

Listen to the Word of God, which is the foundation for what we are after—authentic power. It was spoken through a power seeker named Paul many years ago:

> I want to know Christ and the *power of his resurrection* and the fellowship of sharing in his sufferings, becoming like him in his death, and so, somehow, to attain to the resurrection from the dead. Not that I have already obtained all this, or have already been made perfect, but I press on to take hold of that for which Christ Jesus took hold of me. Brothers, I do not consider myself yet to have taken hold of it. But one thing I do: Forgetting what is behind and straining toward what is ahead, I press on toward the goal to win the prize for which God has called me heavenward in Christ Jesus. (Philippians 3:10–14)

Whether I am in the Middle East, in my office, or at home with my family, I want to live like this. And I can! You can too. How can I be so sure? Because I am always sure about God's promises. In the midst of all that I do not understand in this world, the promises of God have always been the strong wind of clarity to blow away the dust clouds of confusion. When I trust nothing else, I can trust His promises.

GOD'S POWER PROMISE

Young Elisabeth Elliot watched her husband, Jim, board the small plane along with four other missionaries. She had come to Ecuador for this moment. As she stood with her friends, the wives of the other four men, she knew that it could be the last time she saw her husband on this earth. And it was.

The missionaries were flying into the jungle in an attempt to reach the Aucas, one of the fiercest and most dangerous tribes on earth. They had killed every outsider who had tried to make contact with them. And they killed these five as well, spearing them to death. Their deaths would lead to the eventual evangelization of the entire tribe and to an explosive increase in new missionaries. But their deaths also left behind five widows.

The year was 1956, and it was not the last time Elisabeth Elliot would face grief and loss. Another husband would die in the years ahead. And yet after it all, almost half a century later, she would write:

> Life holds for all of us, from time to time, desolate places.... Don't despair. Even though you find no signs, be sure that thousands have traversed this terrain. When you reach the far side you will meet them. But there is something far more comforting than that. You are *not* alone *now*. Always beside you is Another whose voice you may not hear, whose arm you may not feel, whose footprint you may not see. Nevertheless, His Word is utterly to be trusted.[1]

Yes! His Word is utterly to be trusted! And it is there we find His promises.

And God *has* promised us power. It does not come from a Harvard MBA, from top-notch corporate experience, from the title of president or king. The kind of power God promises comes only from Him. It is a gift. And it is so important to Him that Jesus promised it to His followers in the last thing He said before He ascended to heaven and launched His church into the world:

> "But you will receive power when the Holy Spirit comes on you." (Acts 1:8)

If you are a follower of Jesus, you already have all the power you need! If you question that, be patient. I think you'll find some answers in the first chapter. There we'll see that our real problem is not that we don't have power, but that we don't *know* we have it. And that's where Philippians 3:10–14 comes in.

All of God's Word is a life map. We don't often live like it is and that's a big mistake. No one should be in a vast wilderness without a map. And in a world utterly confused about authentic power, and completely blind to the reality of the resurrection realm, this passage is a map to find power—to *know* power. To follow the map will require a journey like none you've ever taken before. If you are ready, we can begin that journey now. It's a journey worth taking. Because the destination will be all the power you need for the rest of your life and beyond. The destination is authentic power!

PART ONE:

RECOGNIZING THE REALM OF THE RESURRECTION

Power, I said. Power to walk into the gold vaults of the nations, into the secrets of kings, into the holy of holies. Power to make multitudes run squealing in terror at the touch of my little invisible finger. Even the moon's frightened of me. Frightened to death. The whole world's frightened to death.

THE INVISIBLE MAN EXPLAINS HIS PLANS
THE INVISIBLE MAN BY R. C. SHERRIFF, 1933

CHAPTER ONE

A DOORWAY FOR THE DESPERATE

I want to know Christ and the power of his resurrection.

PHILIPPIANS 3:10

There *are* frightening things in the invisible world. There's a reason why as children we were afraid of what was under the bed and why even as adults a moonlit stroll through an old graveyard doesn't appeal to us. Inherently, we know another dimension exists. More than what we see is there, and some of what we don't see is frightening indeed. Terrifying, dark power. Evil.

Because the realm of the resurrection is also a part of the invisible world, we may fear it at first. But the most terrifying thing of all is to miss the invisible world altogether. Because the only power *over evil* is found there as well. And a power that is wonderful beyond words is there. A gift that will transform life as we know it in the visible world.

Few go there though. Fewer still learn to live there—to walk every moment simultaneously in two worlds. One seen and one unseen. It is just so much easier to focus our lives on what we can touch and hold on to. To keep living in a fantasy world that seems like reality, and that keeps assuring us that what we don't understand doesn't matter and can't be understood anyway.

To recognize the resurrection realm and learn to live in it usually requires desperation. Something happens that shakes us, scares us, or amazes us. Our routine is shattered. We get sick, or the one we love the most does. Or we get healed and know that no doctor could have done it. It can be something wonderful or something terrible, but suddenly we see it—that life will never make sense, never be fully lived unless it means more than that really cool car or really great vacation we've been working so hard for. We need the invisible, and we'll do almost anything to find it.

Maybe that's why you're reading this book. Something has happened to you. Something that has left you powerless or desperately in need of real power. Once in a while that desperation develops gradually in someone. The stuff of life piles up for so long that the gnawing hunger just won't go away—there has to be something more! Something unseen. And there is. There is a doorway into that realm—but it is a doorway for the desperate.

OPENING THE DOOR

Jesus opened the door. Not a supernatural door. Not a heavenly door. Just a plain old wooden door. In a city called Nazareth. He stepped out into the dusty village street and turned and closed the door—for the last time. The decision was made and the mission begun. The next three years would take Him away from everything on this earth He knew—His family, His work, His home. Ultimately, the journey would lead Him from all that was familiar into something He had never been familiar with at all—sin. He had never experienced it, never tasted the foul flavor of disobedience to His Father. But now He would taste it. All of it. All that had ever been or ever would be. He would be immersed in it, crushed and consumed by it. He would *become* sin on the cross. And as He opened the door to begin the journey that would lead Him there, He already knew His destination!

Why would He do such a thing? A desperate heart drove Him. Not some uncontrolled, unplanned desperation. A desperate love—a love for you. Jesus knew that unless He conquered sin and death, there would be no life for us. No hope. And He loved us too much to let that happen.

Every great journey begins by opening a door. Do you ever in your life *remember* opening a door? And closing it behind you? If you do, it was probably the beginning of a journey. The only time I distinctly remember opening and closing a door was in August of 1978. I looked around my room one last time, opened the door, walked out, and closed it behind me. I stood there and stared at the door for a moment. It suddenly struck me that I would never do that again. I was leaving my North Carolina home and driving to Texas to begin college. Even then I had no idea how that journey would change my life. If you choose to open the door into the invisible realm, you most certainly will not forget it. And nothing will ever be the same.

Paul found that out on a road that led to Damascus. The invisible realm suddenly entered his visible world, and he closed the door on his old life forever. He turned away from all of the earthly power he had possessed and became a desperate seeker of the authentic power of the resurrection. And many years later, sitting in a Roman prison, he was still a desperate man. But not desperate to get out. He had been in chains before and knew that he likely would be again. He was desperate to know more of the life of God's power. And out of that desperation, he prepared to write the words that are the heart of this book, the foundation of authentic power.

TRADING IT ALL AWAY

But whatever was to my profit I now consider loss for the sake of Christ. What is more, I consider everything a loss compared to the surpassing greatness of knowing Christ Jesus my Lord, for whose sake I have lost all things. I consider them rubbish, that I may gain Christ. (Philippians 3:7–8)

What an amazing statement!

Paul had it all—prestige, worldly power, position, even Roman citizenship. Yet he said that all the profit he had once sought now seemed like loss. What's more, he claimed that he considered *everything* else worthless. Everything he could have possibly achieved and gained for himself. Not just what he had, but unlimited potential to get more. It was all loss, he said, worthy only to be traded for one thing.

In fact, Paul felt so strongly about this that he called all he was trading away "rubbish." This word isn't used anywhere else in the Bible. It's a pretty nasty word. Greek scholar A. T. Robertson says it either means "dung" or "dog food." It may have meant both. In those days, before sewage systems, the household bucket had to be emptied somewhere. In it might be both table scraps and human waste. Where it was emptied the dogs would gather for a meal. Yuck! But that's what Paul said everything in life was like to him compared to the one thing he was really after. What was worth so much—everything—to him? He had already said it once, but now he pours it out. Perhaps in that prison cell, he shouted it, rattling the chains with his desperation: *"I want to know Christ"* (Philippians 3:10).

That's what he would trade everything for. But are we to believe that after all Paul's years of following Christ, he didn't know Him yet? Well, that brings us to one of the most important things we'll see in this book. This could change you if you're ready—if you're desperate.

KNOWING CHRIST

What does *knowing Christ* really mean? "You know Tom Davis, don't you?"

"Isn't he the guy who works in shipping?"

"No, Tom's in sales."

"Oh yeah, I met him at the office party last month. I *know* him."

We've all had that conversation, haven't we? Is that what it means to know Christ? That we have some vague knowledge of who He is, but no real relationship? Or does it mean that we received Him as our Savior at some point, were born again, and will spend forever with Him in heaven?

It doesn't mean either of these!

The Bible uses different words that we translate "to know." Of course Paul had met Christ. He certainly had received Him as his Savior. He wrote many of the great passages in the Bible that help us understand salvation. But this word means something different, something deeper. This word doesn't mean to recognize, to have acquaintance with, or to know intuitively; it means to know by continuing experience, to know what cannot be known through the senses, *to know Him in the invisible world!* The *Complete Biblical Library* says that the word means "to see things as they truly are."

It is one of the most mysterious and intimate words of the Greek language or any other language. It is even used in the Bible to describe sex, that most intimate "knowing" between a man and a woman (Luke 1:34, KJV). It is to know someone as no one else can be known. This is what Paul was so desperate for. This is what he meant when he said he wanted to know Christ. He longed to see Him as He truly was, not to hear about Him, not to learn more facts. But to *know* Him. This is the way he thought about God. And that is so important for you to understand and consider in your own life.

A. W. Tozer said, "Were we able to extract from any man a complete answer to the question, 'What comes into your mind when you think about God?' we might predict with certainty the spiritual future of that man."[2] When Paul thought about God, he was desperate to know Him as He really was, to daily meet Him where most people would never go. And so his life was filled with a power most people know nothing about.

What comes to your mind when you think about God? Is there any desperation there—to really *know* Him? Because you *can* really know Him. That knowledge is not reserved for apostles. Jesus said so. "I am the good shepherd; I know my sheep and my sheep know me—just as the Father knows me and I know the Father—and I lay down my life for the sheep" (John 10:14–15). "My sheep *know* me"—same word! He wants you to know Him, not just like Paul knew Him, but as the Father and the Son know each other. Amazing! And what's more, He knows you—the real you, the unseen you. Even things you have not yet seen about yourself.

When we think of God knowing us this way, we are more likely to be terrified than happy. "If He knows everything about me, then He knows…" Yes, He knows *that*! What no one else knows. What might He do to me if He knows everything?

My friend Rich was with me on a trip to the Middle East. He spent a few days with a tribe of Bedouin shepherds in Syria. Rich thought he would use the Parable of the Lost Sheep to share Christ with one of the shepherds who had no knowledge of the gospel. He asked him what he would do if he had a hundred sheep and one of them wandered away. The shepherd immediately said that he would leave the others and go find the lost sheep. Just like Jesus! Rich could see the evangelistic opportunity coming. He asked the shepherd how he would feel when he found the lost sheep. The shepherd replied that he would be so angry the stupid sheep had wandered away that he would cook him for dinner! Rich immediately changed evangelistic strategies.

We tend to think of Jesus as this kind of shepherd.

Why would He let us know Him in this powerful way when we have failed Him so many times, when we wander away as if we do not care if we even know Him at all? Because this Shepherd lays down His life for wandering sheep. He did it knowing full well that we would wander. He did it so we could *know* Him.

That knowledge waits for you. Jesus told His followers, "The knowledge of the secrets of the kingdom of heaven has been given to you" (Matthew 13:11). You already have it! The only question is whether you are desperate enough to begin to know what you have.

GASPING AFTER GOD

George Whitefield, the great preacher and leader of the first spiritual awakening in America, once preached a sermon on Philippians 3. It was a masterpiece. In the conclusion of his message, Whitefield explained just how we are to live out this passage, how we are to know Christ in the way He invites us to. In a mighty voice he commanded followers of Christ to "be continually gasping after God."[3]

Gasping after God. I think that sums it up well.

Occasionally I go snorkeling, though I much prefer

scuba diving. When I snorkel, I am always a little frustrated that I cannot get a close-up view of the reef. I feel called deeper. So I fill my lungs with all the air I can suck in and dive down. Inevitably, I'll stay down there just a little too long. Then I'll look up at the surface maybe twenty feet away and shoot for it. My lungs will burn as I fin as powerfully as I can, my brain screaming for oxygen. As I finally break the surface, I throw my head back and take in air, all of it that I can get. I gasp. Again and again. At that moment, I want nothing more.

God waits for me and you to gasp for Him like this. This is knowing Him. And as Tozer said in *The Knowledge of the Holy,* "If we would bring back spiritual power to our lives, we must begin to think of God more nearly as He is."[4] So let's think together of who He really is, and of the wonder that we can know Him! For who or what you are desperate to know will determine the kind of power you will have in this life.

OPENING THE DOOR TO POWER

Paul wanted to know something very specific about Christ. In fact, it was the reason he was so desperate, the reason he was gasping after God. He wanted to know

Christ's power. "I want to know Christ and the *power* of his resurrection" (Philippians 3:10). He said these things in such a way that they can't be separated. If he was going to know Christ, it would have to be in His resurrection power. There was no other way to really know Him. There's no other way for us either. So what does it mean? What is this power of His resurrection that we are after?

The word *power* is clearly one of the most important words in the Bible. It is used more than 120 times, and Peter tells us that "His divine *power* has given us everything we need for life and godliness" (2 Peter 1:3). Anything that gives me *everything I need* is something I want to know about! Jesus said it's a serious mistake to miss it: "Are you not in error because you do not know the Scriptures or the *power* of God?" (Mark 12:24).

The Greek word for power is *dunamis,* from which we derive our word *dynamite*. And everywhere you find Jesus in the Bible, you will find power exploding off the page. For example, He was conceived in power—in Luke 1:35, the angel Gabriel says to Mary, "The Holy Spirit will come upon you, and the *power* of the Most High will overshadow you."

His ministry was filled with power from beginning to end:

- He taught and lived in power. "Jesus returned to Galilee in the power of the Spirit, and news about him spread through the whole countryside" (Luke 4:14).

- He healed in power. "And the power of the Lord was present for him to heal the sick" (Luke 5:17).

- When His power went from Him to others, He knew it immediately. "At once Jesus realized that power had gone out from him" (Mark 5:30).

- He died in power. "The message of the cross is…the power of God" (1 Corinthians 1:18).

- He was raised in power. "By his power God raised the Lord from the dead, and he will raise us also" (1 Corinthians 6:14).

- He is returning in power. "At that time men will see the Son of Man coming in clouds with great power and glory" (Mark 13:26).

- Everything that exists is under His power. "Jesus knew that the Father had put all things under his power" (John 13:3).

Are you starting to see why Paul was so desperate to know power—and why we should join him?

But caution is in order. To be a power seeker is

dangerous business. There are other powers in this world. Dangerous powers. Powers not to be sought but to either flee or overcome. In my book *The Passion Promise*, I discussed how to use God's power in the battles we face. We must not forget that our battle is "against the powers of this dark world" (Ephesians 6:12). There is a great danger in invisible places, even near the resurrection realm. A darkness that often looks like light can attract even followers of Jesus like moths to a deadly flame. "For Satan himself masquerades as an angel of light" (2 Corinthians 11:14).

For many of us, there is a certain unusual pull in our lives by the risky, the dangerous. This is not necessarily a bad thing, as it can free us to follow Jesus whenever and wherever He leads. But we must be on our guard. Our dark and powerful enemy can make deadly evil look enticingly like exciting risk.

I have been amazed recently to find that more than one of my friends has become involved in the dark side of power. I'm not talking about my friends who don't know Christ. I'm talking about Christian friends—in one case, one of the most effective Christian leaders I have ever known. Involved in demonic things, even consulting demons themselves! I know this is hard to believe, but it is happening.

I asked this friend how in the world this came about. He told me he had decided there was something he wanted in life that God had not given him; he wanted it so badly he would do anything to get it, even call on Satan himself. He said, "John, the cost of this has been greater than anything anyone could ever imagine." The tragedy of his decision broke my heart. But it also reminded me that there is danger in seeking power. A slight shift in my heart can lead to disaster.

I wrote part of this book in the Bahamas while on a scuba diving/writing getaway. One morning we dove a shipwreck off the coast of New Providence Island. As I approached the ship, I saw a large Caribbean reef shark coming directly toward me. Now, I know that this sounds terrifying, but most divers hope to see sharks. It's a fairly rare event, and sharks almost never bother divers. I had seen reef sharks before and had never had the slightest problem with them. I was excited to see this shark.

But then the shark lowered its fins in a typically aggressive posture and charged me! The shipwreck we were diving was called the Ray of Hope, and suddenly I thought I had none. But just a few yards before it reached me, the shark opened its toothy mouth and munched a fish.

After crawling *back* into my wetsuit, I found myself

laughing underwater. The shark wasn't interested in eating me—this time. But it was a good reminder. Where there is power, there is always danger.

Paul gives us foolproof protection against seeking the wrong kind of power. It wasn't just *any* power he was after. It was the "power of his resurrection." Resurrection power! Pursue that power and you will never be confused by counterfeits, because there is no other power like it. After all, no one else has it but Jesus. No one else ever rose! Jesus said, "I *am* the resurrection and the life" (John 11:25). When we are pursuing resurrection power, we are always safe because we are seeking the resurrected one! It is our privilege and family inheritance to pursue resurrection power. Jesus calls us "children of the resurrection" (Luke 20:36). It's time for every believer to throw open the door to this power!

EXACTLY WHAT WE'RE AFTER

It's time for us to clearly define power—the power Paul wanted so badly to know, the power we're after too. To do that, we need to look at some incredible words from Ephesians 1:18–20. Paul makes it clear that God's purpose for us is to know His power, His promise. Then he tells us exactly what that power is.

> I pray also that the eyes of your heart may be
> enlightened in order that you may know the hope to
> which he has called you, the riches of his glorious
> inheritance in the saints, and his *incomparably great*
> *power for us who believe.*

There it is! His power is great beyond compare, and He wants us to *know* that power every day. This is significant; power is *"for us."* It was very rare in the Old Testament for anyone to *have* God's power. They could see it, and it would even come upon them for a time, but they could not have it. But all that has changed now. The empty tomb became the faucet of God's power pouring out on every believer. It is now the *normal* state for a believer to have power. It is *for* us! Listen as Paul defines power for us:

> That power is like the working of his mighty
> strength, which he exerted in Christ when he
> *raised him from the dead.*

When we talk about resurrection power, we are not talking symbolically. We don't mean power that reminds us of the resurrection or teaches us about the resurrection.

We're talking about the actual power that raised Jesus! And the power He had as He came out of the tomb.

Now remember—and this is so important—if you are a follower of Jesus, you already have this power! Jesus said so in Acts 1:8. When His Spirit comes on you, He always brings power. And the Bible makes it clear that the Spirit has come upon every believer. That's what makes us believers! Only through the Spirit of God can a person be born again. Paul says in Romans 8:9, "And if anyone does not have the Spirit of Christ, he does not belong to Christ." If you are His, then His power is yours. Unbelievable!

Our goal is not to get power or to increase our power, but to *know* the power we have. To know it by experience. To live in God's invisible dimension of power while we walk in this visible world. So let's put this all together and see the definition of authentic power. Here it is: God's promise to you.

AUTHENTIC POWER

You have the ability to live every moment in the same strength Jesus had as He stepped out of the tomb.

You can't see this power. You can't hold it, touch it, earn it, drive it, build it, or achieve it. But you can *know* it. You can live in this realm. By the way, the word *realm* means kingdom. You can live every moment in the kingdom where the power of His resurrection rules! And that's what we're going to talk about for the rest of this book, using Philippians 3:10–14 as our life map.

What if resurrection power became normal for the church again? It once was, you know. The book of Acts is that story. Resurrection power was so normal and pervasive throughout the New Testament church that it could not be resisted. It changed history. I have come to believe that if power ever pervades the church again, it won't occur through institutions or organizations. It will only happen through a movement. That's what the New Testament church was—a movement of resurrection power. Movements require leaders and models to look to. Could it be that God is looking for some of His people today to be those leaders—to be models of authentic power for the church to see?

I believe that Bill Bright was one of the greatest men who ever lived. He said it well: "If I am controlled and empowered by Christ, He will be walking around in my body, living His resurrection life in and through me." It wouldn't take many living that way to spark the mighty movement of power we so desperately need in this world.

But it has to be experienced! It's been so long since power has really been the DNA of the church.

I love the NCAA basketball tournament. March Madness. There's nothing like it. I'll never forget the 1983 national championship game. No one who saw it ever will. North Carolina State won in a huge upset in a last-second miracle. Head coach Jim Valvano went absolutely nuts. He ran across the court, leaping on everyone in sight. He talked about his reaction later.

> All the other coaches win the national championship, they button their coat, they go shake hands with their opponent. This guy goes out of his tree. Why? Because all of my life I had grown up watching *Wide World of Sports*. Remember what the agony of defeat was? The skier. But the joy of victory. They don't have one. I was going to give 'em one![5]

The world has gone far too long without a model of the victory found in resurrection power. Let's give them one! "Where is the power of the resurrection?" my friend Gary asked. Let it be in us! That's something worth being desperate for. Let's go through the doorway for the desperate together and slam it behind us forever on anything less than authentic power.

CHAPTER TWO

FINDING RESURRECTION POWER IN RAW PAIN

...and the fellowship of sharing in his sufferings.

PHILIPPIANS 3:10

Father, make us more like Jesus. Help us bear diffi-culty, pain, disappointment, and sorrow, knowing that in Your perfect working and design You can use such bitter experiences to mold our characters and make us more like our Lord. We look with hope to the day when we will be completely like Christ, because we will see Him as He is.... My passions are crucified, there is no heat in my flesh, and a stream flows murmuring inside me, deep down inside me, saying, "Come to the Father."

PRAYER OF ST. IGNATIUS, ROME, a.d. 111,
BEFORE BEING KILLED BY LIONS

M y adventures with electricity are legendary among those who know me well. I have had so many unfortunate high-voltage encounters that no one in my church is shocked anymore when I'm…well, shocked. Recently I was cleaning out a closet in our basement. It had accumulated a lot of clutter in the seven years we've lived there, and it took me a while to get to the bottom of the pile. It was Saturday, and I was wearing my official day-off uniform—raggedy shorts, a nine-year-old T-shirt, and no shoes. As I moved the last bit of junk, some old metal chairs, I hit the side of my right foot on something on the floor. And the next thing I knew I found myself on my back, staring at the ceiling just outside the closet.

My son was sitting on the floor concentrating on the PlayStation. He looked at me as if I had lost my mind. "Dad, what are you doing?"

As I lay there contemplating his question, the brilliant thought occurred to me that I must have hit some bizarre pressure point on my foot that knocked me down. I peered into the closet to find the object that had attacked me and saw a three-prong rolled-up extension cord lying there. "Hey Trey, look at this. I hit my foot on this plug and it knocked me down. If anyone ever tries to hurt you, kick them in the side of the foot. It's like some kind of martial arts nerve center."

He looked at the cord. "Dad, maybe it just shocked you."

Kids can be so dumb. I pointed at the cord and proceeded to give my son a lesson on electrical cords. "Son, don't you know this is the male end of the cord? There's no current in this. It's not even plugged in. See?" And I grabbed the prongs....

Things are a little fuzzy after that. Other than the hysterical laughter of my son, nothing seemed to register for a few minutes. After things cleared up, I carefully investigated the situation. The builder of our house had installed a 220-volt cord wired directly into the wall, apparently for use with some sort of generator. For all those years, I had never even known it was there. But I know it now!

How strange that it took such pain for me to know the power source was there! But the same thing is true in our lives. Though it isn't pleasant and we would like it to be otherwise, the road to resurrection power is paved with pain. If we want to live in the power Jesus had as He came out of the tomb, then we must also expect to share in the sufferings He experienced before He went in. Even so, "the fellowship of sharing in his sufferings" have to be among the deepest, most mystical words of the Bible. They seem just slightly out of reach of our full understanding.

Yet if we seek authentic power, we must seek to understand them, to live in them. C. S. Lewis had a good understanding of God's ways when he said, "God whispers to us in our pleasures, speaks in our conscience, but shouts in our pain. Pain is His megaphone to rouse a deaf world." This whole concept seems foreign to us because our lives are so aligned around avoiding pain and maintaining control. Pain takes away our control, and it is hard for us to see the power in that.

One of my favorite people in the world is a man in our church named Mario. Mario recently became a follower of Christ and before that had been an alcoholic for many years. His wife prayed for him for a long time. He had never been in a church and never read the Bible. He had never known any of the joys of fellowship with God's people. When he first came to Christ, he discovered a whole new world. He came to Wednesday dinners where everyone acted like family. He sat enthralled on Sundays listening to music he had never heard before. He made real friendships for the first time in his life. And everywhere he went, someone hugged him!

I found him walking around our dining room with tears in his eyes one Wednesday night just after he had come to Christ. With a strange mixture of joy and regret he said, "I can't believe I missed all this for fifty years!"

As I was writing this chapter, Mario talked to me

about the change in his life. He said, "I can't believe that I actually have the power now to control my life. As long as I tried to keep control of it, I was always out of control. But when I gave away my control, I got control!"

That's a pretty good theology of power. We have been conditioned to believe that the more control we have over circumstances, the more power we will have. But when pain enters our life, we often have no control at all. Then our life can be an open channel for the power of God to flow in us and through us.

Remember, as God's children we already have all the power we need within us. Pain is God's scalpel that cuts away the hard, dead thickness of our souls so the power can flow from us. We need to know how to live in that power no matter what pain comes our way. And by now, we should know where to look for our answers

REAL LIFE IN THE RESURRECTION REALM

Living in the power Jesus had as He stepped out of the tomb is not some vague theological concept to ponder. It is the key to living with strength and joy in the dirt and grime of the real world. And never was there a dirtier or grimier world than that of the New Testament church. We need to look back at their day and learn from their lives. They were living in the afterglow of the resurrection. The resurrection realm was real to them—it was their world, their kingdom. Everything in their lives was seen through the lens of the resurrection. Even suffering.

When the leaders of the first Jesus-followers were arrested and beaten for proclaiming Jesus, this was their response: "The apostles left the Sanhedrin, rejoicing because they had been counted worthy of suffering disgrace for the Name. Day after day, in the temple courts and from house to house, they never stopped teaching and proclaiming the good news that Jesus is the Christ" (Acts 5:41–42). How did they know that Jesus was the Christ, the Messiah? Because they had seen Him risen! And more than that, they had risen with Him. His power was in them. Suffering and disgrace were now a channel of power for them.

Paul was even stronger about the power found through suffering.

Join with me in suffering for the gospel, by the power of God, who has saved us and called us to a holy life—not because of anything we have done but because of his own purpose and grace. This grace was given us in Christ Jesus before the beginning of time, but it has now been revealed by the appearing of our Savior, Christ Jesus, who has destroyed death and has brought life and immortality to light through the gospel. (2 Timothy 1:8–10)

Did you get all that? Paul actually *invites* people to suffer with him and to do it by God's power. And he reminds everyone that the grace to do this comes from the one who destroyed death—from the resurrection realm. And he concludes by declaring that all this is *good news*— the gospel. Good news, suffering. That's what the New Testament church believed. That's how they lived.

But why should *we* want to live that way? Are we supposed to be spiritual masochists who get some sick thrill out of suffering? Of course not. But the truth is that we can't avoid suffering. We are in a fallen world. And making it our goal to avoid suffering is surprisingly painful itself. As Thomas Merton said, "The truth that many people never understand, until it is too late, is that the more you try to avoid suffering the more you suffer because smaller and more insignificant things begin to torture you in proportion to your fear of being hurt."

There is a better way to approach suffering. We cannot determine not to suffer, but we can determine what it will mean. This is the New Testament pattern. And this was the early Christ-followers' key to living in resurrection power—and ours.

STRATEGIC SUFFERING

The first Christ-followers would find our comfortable Christianity an alien landscape. Their faith was birthed, nourished, and flourished in pain—often raw, unrelenting pain. But this was not a surprise to them. "Dear friends, do not be surprised at the painful trial you are suffering, as though something strange were happening to you" (1 Peter 4:12).

G. K. Chesterton said that New Testament believers are promised three things: "to be completely fearless, absurdly happy, and in constant trouble."[6] We like the first two of those promises, but want to avoid the third. The first believers were content with the whole package, and even more, they believed in suffering strategically—in joining God's work in the middle of suffering, in finding His purpose there and even His advantageous strategy of using suffering in our lives. Suffering believers today can make the same choice. And when we do, we will find God's authentic power there—and some wonderful gifts to go with it.

THE GIFT OF PURPOSE

When we suffer, our biggest question is why? My greatest doubts and struggles in ministry have surrounded this question. When I have watched some of God's most wonderful servants suffer and die what seem to be prematurely, I have wondered at God's wisdom. But these same experiences have also provided the greatest strength to my faith, for in the most intense suffering, I have seen over and over again God's amazing purpose. God *does* answer the "why" question. He doesn't give a detailed analysis of your individual suffering, but He does tell you why it is happening. It's happening so that His authentic power can be fulfilled in your life. He is working His huge purpose in you.

Paul wrote, "But he said to me, 'My grace is sufficient for you, for my power is made perfect in weakness.' Therefore I will boast all the more gladly about my weaknesses, *so that Christ's power may rest on me*" (2 Corinthians 12:9). That's big! It is only in your weakness, in your suffering, that His power becomes perfect in you, that His power rests on you. That is why! And when we really begin to believe that, and to know that God is always taking the thousand-year look when we are taking the present moment look, we can trust Him with our suffering and rest in His purpose for it.

As I was writing this chapter I met a woman in the midst of great suffering—a woman of amazing purpose and power. Kathy is new to our church. She just moved here with her three children following the death a year ago of her forty-six-year-old husband from cancer. As she shared with grace and courage about her wonderful husband and the pain of his loss, I was amazed by her response to suffering. She said, "I miss my husband so much, but I know beyond any doubt that my calling is now to raise my children so that their lives count like their father's did—and so that they will touch other lives as well."

I wept with her as she told me of her nine-year-old son's response to the first anniversary of his father's death: "Mom, we are one year closer to seeing Daddy again."

She then told me that her young son had two questions in life: Why did God take his daddy, and why are there ants?

I couldn't help much with the second one, but we talked about the first. "Kathy," I said, "I don't know all of the details of God's plan, but I want you to know this. I intend to write about your suffering in a book. Could God, who weeps with you now, allow this pain because He knows that one person may read your story and not give in to despair in their own suffering? And if that one person became a tool in the hands of God to reach thousands for His kingdom, would God in His great love for the world allow your loss for that purpose?" We agreed to pray in faith for that very thing. Maybe *you* are that reader! I can't wait to find out the details in heaven, but neither Kathy nor I doubt God's purpose in pain. And you don't have to either.

THE GIFT OF STRENGTH AND SIGNIFICANCE

If God said to you, "I want to give you all the strength you will ever need and fill your life with significant meaning," you would jump on that offer, wouldn't you? Well, He does say that. But the channel God uses to bring it to you is suffering.

"And the God of all grace, who called you to his eternal glory in Christ, after you have suffered a little while, will himself restore you and make you strong, firm and steadfast" (1 Peter 5:10). God *Himself* will do this! What an amazing promise. And it makes perfect sense. How can

God give us strength that we do not need? Suffering brings us into dependence on God, and it is there that we find Him to be all we need. It is there that we are sculpted into the shape that will fit into God's greater plan to give us a mind-blowingly significant life!

Again, the New Testament church had this figured out because they accepted suffering as strategic in their lives. Paul wrote from prison,

> Now I want you to know, brothers, that what has happened to me has really served to advance the gospel. As a result, it has become clear throughout the whole palace guard and to everyone else that I am in chains for Christ. Because of my chains, most of the brothers in the Lord have been encouraged to speak the word of God more courageously and fearlessly. (Philippians 1:12–14)

What a wonderfully clear picture of significance in suffering. There is no despair in this life as deep as suffering with no significance. But that is an impossibility for God's children! He never wastes your pain. God is always at work to call people to Himself, and the world's ability to see how Christians suffer is one of His greatest tools.

The persecuted church today understands this as well as they did two thousand years ago. In the remarkable book *The Heavenly Man,* Brother Yun, one of the key leaders of the revival in China, says:

Once I spoke in the West and a Christian told me, "I've been praying for years that the Communist government in China will collapse, so Christians can live in freedom." This is not what we pray! We never pray against our government or call down curses on them. Instead, we have learned that God is in control of both our own lives and the government we live under. Isaiah prophesied about Jesus, "The government will be on his shoulders" (Isaiah 9:6). God has used China's government for his own purposes, molding and shaping his children as he sees fit. Instead of focusing our prayers against any political system, we pray that regardless of what happens to us, we will be pleasing to God. Don't pray for the persecution to stop! We shouldn't pray for a lighter load to carry but a stronger back to endure! Then the world will see that God is with us, empowering us to live in a way that reflects his love and power. That is true freedom![7]

Wow! That's what we're after. That's the power of God that can be found in suffering. And not just in the lives of persecuted believers—but in your life. Trust God with your suffering. He is bringing you strength and significance. Corrie ten Boom said it well: "When a train goes through a tunnel and it gets dark, you don't throw away the ticket and jump off. You sit still and trust the engineer." If you are in the darkness right now, there is power there—because the Engineer is at the controls.

THE GIFT OF JOY

I never cease to be amazed at joyous sufferers, but I am no longer surprised. I have seen them everywhere and in every kind of pain through the years. They are a testimony to the truth of God's Word as they join the millions of believers who have suffered with joy since the days of the early church.

James said, "Consider it pure joy, my brothers, whenever you face trials of many kinds" (James 1:2). Peter said it: "In this you greatly rejoice, though now for a little while you may have had to suffer grief in all kinds of trials" (1 Peter 1:6–7). Paul said it in chains: "Rejoice in the Lord always. I will say it again: Rejoice!" (Philippians 4:4). And they were all following the Lord's teaching:

"Blessed are you when people insult you, persecute you and falsely say all kinds of evil against you because of me. Rejoice and be glad" (Matthew 5:11–12).

One of the greatest privileges of my life has been to witness the joy of the persecuted church in several different countries. Many of the people I have met in Asia, the former Soviet Union, and the Middle East have few possessions and little or no hope of that ever changing. They have no chance of career success, no chance of comfort, no chance of popularity, and a great chance of prison or death. And yet they radiate joy.

My friend Mustafa, whose story I told in the introduction, is one such man. He has been in jail four times, he lives very frugally, he is the only follower of Christ in his people group of fifty thousand, and his family wants to kill him. Sound joyous to you? Oh, but he is! I wish you could meet him. He has a smile that lights up the room and the most contagious laugh I have ever heard.

The first time I met Mustafa, I loved him. After a wonderful sharing time, he embraced me and said, "Brother John, I'm so glad I met you now instead of three years ago because then I would have killed you!" And he laughed loud and long.

Just a few months ago, I was with him again. After a

wonderful time together, I said, "Mustafa, I am concerned for you. You are such a bold witness. You share Christ with everyone you meet. So many of us love you, but you have so many enemies. Do you worry about what will happen to you?"

"No, I don't worry," he said. "I know that one day I will probably just disappear. But until then, what a life!"

What a life? *What* life? He has nothing to bring him joy. And that's the point. No *thing* will bring you joy. But as Russian novelist Aleksandr Solzhenitsyn once said, "You can have power over people as long as you don't take everything away from them. But when you've robbed a man of everything, he's no longer in your power." Mustafa lives in *God's* power—and His joy. No one can take that from him. And so he is free. And you can be too.

How can you suffer strategically and have the joy of the persecuted church if you live in comfort as most of us do? Don't wait for someone to take it all away from you. Give it away now! Tell God that everything you have is His and that you want to know what it is to have His joy, which nothing can take away. Reject the culture of materialism. Simplify your life. Ask God to do whatever it takes to bring you to full dependence on Him for joy.

It's a scary prayer, but wouldn't it be worth it to have a joy that *nothing* can take away?

Don't misunderstand. Suffering in itself does not bring power or joy. It is *how* we approach and journey through suffering that can make it strategic, powerful, and even a path to joy. And that journey is not one you can take alone.

PARTNERSHIP SUFFERING

Paul hungered to "know Christ and the power of his resurrection and the *fellowship of sharing in his sufferings*" (Philippians 3:10). He didn't hunger to suffer. But he hungered to know all of Christ. He didn't want to know a sanitized Jesus who would be his buddy to talk to when it was convenient. He wanted to know the real Jesus. And the real Jesus is a sufferer.

The phrase "the fellowship of sharing" is expressed with one word in the Greek language: *koinonia*. It refers to an intimate partnership that can be experienced only by the grace of God. And the amazing thing is that God invites you into that partnership with Him.

Paul says, "God, who has called you into fellowship with his Son Jesus Christ our Lord, is faithful"

(1 Corinthians 1:9). And He is faithful to invite you to know *all* of Him. "May the grace of the Lord Jesus Christ and the love of God, and the fellowship of the Holy Spirit be with you all" (2 Corinthians 13:14). You are invited into partnership with the love of the Father, with the sacrifice of the Son, and you can share in the very Spirit of God. But you must be willing for that partnership to include His sufferings. It is a package deal.

God *wants* you. He loves you desperately and wants you to share in His sufferings not to hurt you, but to empower you. Dave Dravecky was an All-Star Major League pitcher at the peak of his career when cancer forced the amputation of his pitching arm—a disaster in anyone's book. How has Dravecky responded to this? Has it ruined his life? Listen to what he says:

> When I compare the Dave Dravecky before cancer and the Dave Dravecky after, there's no comparison…. I used to think I could put God's love in a box; now I believe His ways are too deep for any box to contain. I used to depend on myself; now I depend more on God. I used to be preoccupied with my own needs; now I am learning compassion for the needs of others…. Through my own

suffering I have become more aware of [Christ's suffering]. And I love Him more as a result.[8]

This is why God calls you to share in His sufferings. Because it will transform your life and fill you with His power. He wants that for you. And anyone is eligible. "But rejoice that you participate in the sufferings of Christ" (1 Peter 4:13). *Participate.* Same word. To partner with. To share in everything. *Koinonia.*

Do you realize who wrote that verse? The man who would *not* participate in the sufferings of Christ. The man who denied Him three times. The man who ran away and left Jesus alone. And now he was writing the words of Scripture! How did it all change? Because Peter stopped depending on himself and fell with all his weight into a partnership with Jesus. And if Peter was eligible, so are you. Wherever you may find yourself today, no matter how far from the heart of God and His power, it may be time to begin the comeback of your life.

One of the most influential Christians you may have never heard of is Wang Mindao, who spent twenty-two years imprisoned in China for his faith and became one of the most important leaders of the great revival there. Yet early in his life, when threatened with torture by the

Chinese authorities, he agreed to say and preach only what they wanted him to. He wandered the streets of Beijing muttering, "I am Peter. I am Peter." But God was far from through with him. In suffering partnership with Jesus, he made his comeback—all the way back. Today, suffering Christians all over China draw strength from his example. James Hudson Taylor, the grandson of the great missionary Hudson Taylor, wrote, "No Christian Chinese leader in the twentieth century has more clearly articulated the power of the Gospel of Jesus Christ, or more poignantly experienced what the apostle Paul described as *'the fellowship of sharing in his sufferings.'"*

That is God's way—His wonderful, mysterious, powerful way, His way for all of us.

Suffering is coming. That is simply a fact. But as Helen Keller once said, "The world is full of suffering. It is also full of overcoming it." If you want to be one of those overcomers—to turn raw pain into resurrection power like the New Testament believers and the persecuted church today—then trust His strategy. Let Him make your suffering strategic no matter how unfair or impossible it seems. Say with John Henry Newman:

I will trust Him. Whatever, wherever I am, I can never be thrown away. If I am in sickness, my sickness may serve Him; in perplexity, my perplexity may serve Him; if I am in sorrow, my sorrow may serve Him. My sickness, or perplexity, or sorrow may be necessary causes of some great end, which is quite beyond us. He does nothing in vain.[9]

Go ahead, say it. Pray it. And watch His power flow through your pain.

And when the pain is just too intense to bear, and no hope, much less power, is in sight, do what Joni Eareckson Tada does. Speaking to Larry King in August 2004, Joni shared her story of thirty years as a quadriplegic after a diving accident. Though she has been used of God as a speaker, writer, and artist who has touched thousands, she said that each morning is still nearly unbearable—a suffering that is constant and sure to repeat itself tomorrow. Someone has to get her up, wash her, dress her, and take care of her most basic and personal needs. Joni told Larry that often she says, "Lord, I cannot do it today. I have no smile to give to those who will help take care of me. So Jesus, could I borrow Your smile?"

He is your partner in your sufferings—and you in His. His smile is yours. His tears are yours. His power is yours. And the next step you take can be His. Even if it is a step of raw pain, you have His promise that you can take it in the same strength Jesus had in His first step out of the tomb. That's life and painful power in the realm of the resurrection.

CHAPTER THREE

THE DEADLY PATH TO POWER

…becoming like him in his death.

Philippians 3:10

Death is a very dull, dreary affair,
and my advice to you is to have nothing to
do with it.

Somerset Maugham

Death is the most beautiful adventure of life.

Charles Frohman

So which is it? Well, that depends. I sometimes read stories of Christians who look forward to death, but I have never felt that way. I'm excited about what lies *beyond* death—about heaven—but death itself is not my friend. I'll have all of eternity in heaven, but for now God has placed me here, and I want to stay here as long as I can! So if it's *my* death we're talking about, my attitude tends to resonate with Somerset Maugham's.

If it's *your* death we're talking about, it still doesn't seem like an adventure. As a pastor for the last twenty-five years, I have seen more death than I care to remember. The courage and grace with which God's people die never ceases to amaze me, but death itself? It is a fiend, a malevolent hunter that wastes and destroys. It is coughing and gagging, bleeding and crying, struggling and straining for one last breath. I hate it. It robs the people I care about of those they love the most. It brings loneliness, loss, confusion, and fear. I despise it. I hope I have seen my last death and that Jesus will return any minute and render death a moot issue. But until then, I bear no sentimental feelings toward death. He has no friend in me.

The Bible is not very friendly toward death either. "The last enemy to be destroyed is death" (1 Corinthians 15:26). And the best thing about heaven is that "there will be no more death or mourning or crying or pain" (Revelation 21:4). Now *that's* something to look forward to!

Your death or mine is not an adventure; it's a curse. But the death of Another is different. Different from any other death. A death that is as ugly as all the dying I have witnessed and then some, and yet it is no curse. Indeed, it is the breaking of the curse! It is this death, Jesus' death, that so interests Paul. In fact, he makes the stunning claim that he wants to be "like him in his death." And remember, Paul sees this as his path to experiencing authentic power. This dying Jesus is the One he wants to know so desperately.

He's the One I want to know too. But if I am honest, I'm frightened by getting to know Jesus this way. This strange power of His, it is deadly power. Power only known by those who will become acquainted with a cross.

My wife is even a little afraid about me writing this book. "Do you think that all this writing about finding power in suffering and death will mean that you have to experience more of it to write the book?" she asked. An unsettling question. Would I write this book if I knew she was right? Do I really want to know God's power *that much*—like Paul did? If I do, there is no other path but the deadly road of the cross.

MY SON AND HIS SON

October 14, 1990, was a Sunday. I was supposed to be preaching at Northrich Baptist Church in Richardson, Texas, where I was pastor. Instead, I found myself at the hospital with my wife as we awaited the birth of our third child. She was a few weeks early, but nothing that gave us too much concern. We watched different services on television, and I teased her about leaving to preach and then coming right back. We were overjoyed with anticipation. A sonogram had told us that this would be our son. The name was picked out and ready. I am John Paul Avant Jr. He would be John Paul Avant III. We would call him Trey. My two daughters were the joy of my life, but now I was ready for a boy—to play football with, to wrestle with, and to teach to be a man.

As the hours slowly went by, we began to realize with some disappointment that Donna might be experiencing false labor. Her contractions got weaker and farther apart, and we began to prepare ourselves to go home and try this again later. But then an intern came in, and during the examination of my wife, she broke her water without telling us. A few minutes later, we heard our doctor outside the room, asking the intern what she had done. We began to have an uneasy feeling, but our doctor told us not to worry. He would go ahead and induce labor now, and all would be well.

But all was not well. Suddenly our son's heart monitor showed that something was wrong. Doctors and nurses seemed to be running everywhere in the room.

Before we understood what was happening, they were putting my wife to sleep. In fear and confusion she said, "Read Psalm 91," before losing consciousness. Psalm 91 was the chapter she had been memorizing at the time. As my wife was rushed to a surgical room, a nurse explained to me that my son's heart was stopping and they had to get him out immediately to save his life. By the time I got my sterile gown on and ran in to the room, they had cut my wife open and were pulling my son out.

Immediately a team began to work on our little baby to try to get him to breathe. I looked from my son, who was fighting to live, to my wife, lying there unconscious and bleeding, and I fell to my knees. It's hard to explain what happened next. I fully intended to beg God for the life of my son, but another prayer came out instead. I gave my baby boy back to God. I prayed, "Lord, I give you back this precious child. If you have more use for him with You than here with me, I trust You with him."

For what seemed like an hour all I could hear were frantic voices and medical equipment, but then in one of the greatest moments of my life, I heard the sweetest sound I have ever heard—the first cry of my son! Followed by cheers from those who had worked to save his life. He spent days in the ICU but came through the ordeal with no lasting problems. Fourteen years later, he is taller than I am, is my certified scuba buddy, and is a great football player. Psalm 91 is his life passage. We've come a long way since that delivery room.

When I was kneeling on the cold floor of that hospital room, God spoke to me. I had been studying the book of Romans in my devotional life, and as I listened to the first cries of my son and got my first glimpses of him through tear-clouded eyes, a verse from chapter 8 flooded my soul: "He...did not spare his own Son, but gave him up for us all" (v. 32). God had spared my son, but He had not spared His own. I had given my son back to God, and He had chosen to give him back to me. How I love Him for that! And yet with the gift of my son's life came a call— a call I intend to answer. To choose, as I watch my son live, to also watch His die. I want to join Paul and *know* Him, and I can only really know Him as I experience Him on the cross. I can only really become like Him as I am like Him in His death.

Of course I love the One who allowed my son to live. Of course I want to know the power of the God who would give me this gift. But what if my son had died? After all, every day many people have the opposite experience. Their child does not live. Their story does not have a happy ending. Would I still have reason to love Him and know Him if my son had died that day? If I had never heard his little cry? If that had been the case, I cannot imagine the depth of my grief. Perhaps I would have withered into a sorrow from which I would not have recovered. But I hope not. I believe not.

My son's death would not have changed a fundamental fact of our faith. In fact, it would have reinforced it—that into a fallen world where tragedy does claim children, and grief and death often seem to reign supreme, *God so loved the world that He sent His only Son!* Into this world. To die. To not leave us alone in our suffering, but to come to us with His most precious gift and to bear our grief and despair and to break our curse! To ensure that death could not have any of us or our children for long. He *chose* this. And for that, no matter what else occurs, "I want to know Christ, and the power of his resurrection, and the fellowship of sharing in his sufferings, *becoming like him in his death.*"

LIKE HIM

What does that really mean, "Like him in his death"? If we become like Him in His death, what will we be like?

What was *He* like on the cross? And how do we choose
this deadly path to power?

Well, one thing is certainly clear. When the horror of
the cross was finally over, Jesus was dead. Crucifixion was
a one-way ticket. No one survived it. And if we want to be
like Him, we must be dead too. Paul is very specific in
this. The power he seeks doesn't come from just watching
Christ's death or admiring it. It comes from joining it. The
words "becoming like him" mean to be jointly formed. It
is the joining together of two things that cannot be separated. It is something even more significant than the last
breath drawn by a physical body. It is *choosing* the death
of the very essence of ourselves on our own. It is choosing not to be apart from Christ—even on the cross.

We resist death, which I think makes sense. Death is
a horrible thing. I like the last words of murderer James
Rodgers, executed by firing squad. When asked if he had
a last request, he said, "Why, yes. I'd like a bulletproof
vest." That's what most people hope Christianity will be—
a bulletproof vest for life. A ticket to a life where our
wishes are granted and death comes only quietly in our
beds after at least eighty years of comfortable living. But
that's not what God is after for us. He loves us too much
for that. Elisabeth Elliot says:

Our vision is so limited we can hardly imagine a love that does not show itself in protection from suffering.... The love of God did not protect His own Son.... He will not necessarily protect us—not from anything it takes to make us like His Son. A lot of hammering and chiseling and purifying by fire will have to go into the process.[10]

God's desire for us—His goal for our short life here on this earth—is that we not waste it on our own power. On power that is no power at all. He knows what most of us never see. That authentic power comes only to the dead. It is deadly power. Real power looks like this: "For you died, and your life is now hidden with Christ in God" (Colossians 3:3). When all of my ridiculous imitations of power die and my whole life is covered by His, I am hidden by Him. And so the power that He has, I have too!

This is a tough concept to grasp, much less to choose as my life. And the practical implications of it are staggering. As we have seen, this power is already in every believer. But to know it by experience requires that we give up our own life.

Some time ago, I went through a confusing chapter of life. I had a critical decision to make, and I sought the will of God in every way that I knew to seek it. To me, being able to hear God is the most fundamental part of my relationship with Him. If I cannot hear Him, I do not feel qualified to take the next step, much less to lead others. Over time, I became certain that I knew His will. His voice was clear and I was ready to obey.

And then He pulled the rug out from under me.

Nothing I had heard from Him came to pass. My decision was wrong. I felt foolish and strangely misled by God. I did not know which direction to turn next. Nothing made sense.

My best friend saw the state I was in and challenged me in a way I had never heard before. He said, "John, what are you so upset about? You're a dead man! What worry does a dead man have about where they put his body? You gave up your rights to control all this. If God wants you to feel confused for some reason, what is that to you? That's His business."

And he was absolutely right. As time went by, I began to see the whole picture. If I hadn't felt "tricked" by God, I wouldn't have even considered some key directions He actually did want me to go. My own choices would have made a mess of things. Only as I functioned as a dead man, hidden away with Christ, could I live in His power.

So if I want to "become like him in his death," to know His deadly power, what do I do? *I do what Jesus does!* That is always the answer. I join Him. I am "jointly formed" with Him. And what is it that Jesus did on the cross that I am to join? "Your attitude should be the same as that of Christ Jesus: Who, being in very nature God, did not consider equality with God something to be grasped, but made himself nothing" (Philippians 2:5–7). He made Himself nothing. The words mean that he *emptied Himself.* And that is our key. Our agonizing, life-altering, deadly choice. To fill our own lives with all we can, to promote ourselves, to please ourselves, to grab for ourselves all that we can cram into these short years. Or…to die. To empty self into the container called Christ and disappear.

And that is the way God's power works. That's why I call it authentic power. Because God promises us that when we choose to empty ourselves like Jesus—to die with Him—He will never leave us alone. He will invade us. His life *in* us will be better than any life on our own. We will die—but we will not live a dead life! He will fill us with His awesome power because He will fill us with Himself: "I have been crucified with Christ and I no longer live, but Christ lives in me. The life I live in the body, I live by faith in the Son of God, who loved me and gave himself for me" (Galatians 2:20).

That's what authentic power looks like:

I die.

Christ lives in me.

And with Him is all His power. I don't have to seek it. I have it! But if we are going to make this choice to die, it helps to be crystal clear on what power we are trading our life for. If we are to become like Him in His death on the cross, we should ask who He was as He hung there. What power was He wielding on a cross? And since we are asking Him to live through us, what power does He bring into our lives? What is His promise of authentic power? What power is ours?

THE POWER OF A HEALER

Jesus was a healer throughout His ministry, yet it seems that few then or now really understood what that meant. If the main purpose of Jesus' healing was to take away physical disease, then He was a failure. Everyone He healed got sick again and died! But Jesus made it clear that the purpose of His healing was to point us beyond our bodies to the healing of our souls.

No one ever worked as hard to get to Jesus as four men we read about in Mark 2. Their friend was paralyzed and the crowd was thick. So they crawled up on the roof and dug through it (I've often wondered if that was covered by the home owner's insurance). Anyway, after all this work, when they finally got to Jesus, He said something kind of unusual: "Son, your sins are forgiven" (Mark 2:5). Now if I had been one of the guys who razed the roof, I think I would have said, "Thanks, Jesus, but we didn't go to all this trouble for our buddy to get forgiven. We want him healed!"

And, of course, Jesus did make him well. But He also made a critical point. The most important healing has nothing to do with these fragile, temporary bodies that are guaranteed not to stay healed. The essence of healing is forgiveness. Sickness can never hurt me forever. *Sin can.* The most practical thing Jesus can ever do for you is to forgive you. If He heals your sickness, you may still live a ruined life. If He heals your soul, though you may be a regular customer in the ICU, you'll still have all you need for a life of power.

Never was the healing of Jesus so real, so powerful, and so important as it was on the cross. Peter was physically healthy but needed healing when he ran away from the cross where Jesus died. He got that healing, as did we, as Peter tells us: "He himself bore our sins in his body on the tree…by his wounds you have been healed" (1 Peter 2:24). When Jesus said "Father, forgive them" as He hung on the cross, He spoke healing to the world…to the ages, to you, to me.

That is the power that He brings to live in us.

How we need this power! It is the most practical, urgent need of *my* life. As I look around, I see a culture in complete bondage to sin. The very things people are running to for pleasure are eating them alive, destroying them from the inside out. They have all the evidence they need to prove that substance abuse, money, and sex will not fulfill them, but still they are drawn to it all like moths to a flame.

I live in this world. And the terrifying thing is that I am enticed by it all too. I feel the allure. I want the pleasure. Without His power, I know I will self-destruct. But I have it. His power over sin is in me if only I will choose it. "In the same way, count yourselves dead to sin but alive to God in Christ Jesus" (Romans 6:11). I'm alive to God and He has all the power I need.

The sin that frightens me most is sexual sin. It's not that this sin is worse than any other. It's just that the consequences are so disastrous. I would break the heart of my wife and children. I would bring shame and ridicule on the cause of Christ. I would lose my ministry. But here is the really scary thing. I am tempted to do it anyway— every day. After years of counseling and listening to men, I am convinced that I am not alone in this battle. In fact, I really believe there are two kinds of men: those who admit they struggle with sexual temptation and liars. The appeal of a beautiful woman is very real to me. But so is the power of God! And I have seen His power at work in this area, delivering me.

Years ago, God led my wife and me to develop what we call an "emergency plan" in case I am ever in a situation where I am tempted toward an affair. We asked God to give me the strength in that moment to push the button on my cell phone and call my wife. A few years ago, I had to implement the plan.

I was on my way to a conference and was standing on a moving sidewalk in an airport. I heard someone and glanced back. Behind me was a very attractive woman from our church. She was a godly woman and I was happy to see her. "How are you doing?" I said with a big smile. As she looked at me with surprise, I realized to my embarrassment that she was not the woman from my church. She looked just like her, but I had never met this woman before.

She seemed thrilled that I had started a conversation and began to talk about herself. Immediately I felt uncomfortable, but I had no idea what to do about it. As we came to the end of the moving sidewalk, I heard a cracking noise behind me. I turned and saw that the wheel had broken off of the woman's carry-on bag. She was trying to drag it but not making much progress. Looking back, I think a little demon must've been sawing away at that wheel.

I didn't want to be rude, so I offered to carry her bag to her gate. As she continued to talk, I began to get distinct signals that she was flirting with me. It had been so long that I wasn't sure I was picking up the signals correctly, but I was pretty sure this was it. I wish I could tell you that I was disgusted by this turn of events. That, as a man of God, I immediately began to share the gospel with her or something really spiritual like that.

But that didn't happen.

Instead, I enjoyed it. I felt drawn to it. But I also felt some safety in the fact that I was in a public place and about to part ways with this woman. I asked what her gate number was. Same as mine. Uh-oh. I could hear warning bells begin to ring. As we arrived at the gate, I quickly told her how nice it was to meet her and went and sat at a table in a café. As I sat thinking about what had just happened,

I saw out of the corner of my eye that she was coming to my table.

Without asking permission, she sat down, looked me straight in the eye, and said, "Listen, things aren't going too well for me. I don't want to be alone tonight. We're going to the same city. No strings attached. Would you like some company?"

There it was. Right in front of me. Pleasure for the taking.

At that moment I became aware of two things: how beautiful she was sitting there smiling at me, and my cell phone clipped to my belt. I had a choice. Before I could allow myself to think about it or listen to the enemy's mind games, I grabbed my phone and pressed the speed dial for home. "Hi honey," I said. "I don't quite know how to say this, but I'm putting our emergency plan to work. I'm sitting next to a woman who has just invited me to have an affair."

With a tone of voice reminiscent of a martial arts scream, my sweet wife said, "Put her on the phone!" By this time, however, that wasn't necessary. The woman realized this was a mistake, and she quickly left.

After calming my wife and reassuring her of my love (and being reminded that she is excellent with a kitchen knife should I ever make a different choice in this area), I hung up the phone. For a long time thereafter, I could not get two things off my mind. First, that temptation is real and I had a real chance to destroy all that is good in my life. And second, and this quickly overwhelmed my thinking, that *the power of God in me is real.* I can live for Him in this world.

Because it is not me. It is Christ living in me—the Healer! Not just the healer of my body, though I praise him when He does this, but the healer of all that wounds and sickens my soul. The Healer of the sickness of our sinful culture that threatens me with its disease. It is that power, that healing, that I need so much. And that power is available to you every day. It's power worth dying for.

THE POWER OF A LOVER

If Jesus was anything on the cross, He was a lover. Not some silly character from a romantic comedy, but a perfect picture of real, transformational love, offered to you and me as a gift of life and power. "Greater love has no one than this, that he lay down his life for his friends" (John 15:13). And through the cross, Christ brings that love to live inside us. It is a love that cannot really touch us without changing us.

J. B. Phillips said, "God may thunder his commands from Mount Sinai and men may fear, yet remain at heart exactly as they were before. But let a man once see his God down in the arena as a Man, suffering, tempted, sweating, and agonized, finally dying a criminal's death—and he is a hard man indeed who is untouched."[11]

For those who have had the love of Christ come to live within them, there is no possibility at all of being untouched. The power of His love will enable us to do in this world what He did on the cross.

On the cross *He forgave,* and so we have the power to forgive. C. S. Lewis said, "Everyone says forgiveness is a lovely idea until they have something to forgive."[12] It is so difficult to release others from the debt of the hurt they have caused us. It may well be impossible apart from the love of the cross. The powerful, forgiving love Jesus brings to our life looks beyond the pain someone has caused us into the pain of his or her own heart. We then can see them through the eyes of Jesus—with His compassion. Longfellow wrote, "If we could read the secret history of our enemies, we would find in each person's life sorrow and suffering enough to disarm all hostility." What freedom when you are no longer bound to hate and bitterness! That is true power.

On the cross *He sacrificed,* and so we have the power to sacrifice. "Live a life of love," God says, "just as Christ loved us and gave himself up for us as a fragrant offering and sacrifice to God" (Ephesians 5:2). We are driven by the world we live in to do all we can to take care of ourselves. We will be driven by the love and power of God to do all *He* can in us to take care of the needs of others. We will be able to serve sacrificially because we will be serving supernaturally. And the joy that comes in the lives we touch is worth far more than the sacrifice.

On the cross *He loved,* and so we have the power to love. Psalm 136 is one of my favorite chapters in the Bible. The psalmist remembers history—all that God has done and all that His people have faced. And in every one of twenty-six verses he says, "His love endures forever." His love endures because the Lover went to the cross to seal forever the power of that love for us. The world is so confused about what love is and how to find it. But the power of the Lover Jesus will transform our relationships, our families, our marriages, our parenting, our churches, our lives. And that is power worth dying for.

THE POWER OF A WARRIOR

And having disarmed the powers and authorities,
he made a public spectacle of them, triumphing
over them by the cross. (Colossians 2:15)

If ever there was a public spectacle, it was a man on a cross. Hanging naked at a busy intersection for all to see. But no one saw what was really going on when Jesus hung there. The real public spectacle took place in the spiritual realm, where the blood of Jesus stripped away the enemy's best weapons and left him a toothless lion, a swordless adversary. Jesus is a warrior!

This is one of the most important things we can understand about Christ. Most believers don't really get it, but it is important to realize that God is no pacifist. You just can't find it in the Bible. And that's good news, because in this battle we're in I want a warrior on my side. Even the world seems to understand this. An anonymous CIA officer chides America for treating September 11 almost like a celebration:

Would that we relearn to mourn with quiet dignity and to celebrate only when the cause of mourning is eradicated. Our response to attacks should be to bury our dead while confirming our resolve to destroy their killers by reciting grave-side verses from the 144th Psalm: "Blessed be the Lord my strength, which teaches my hands to war and my fingers to fight.... Bow thy heavens, O Lord, and come down; touch the mountains and they shall smoke. Cast forth lightning, and scatter out thine arrows and destroy them.[13]

Strong stuff. But stuff we need in the real world. It is great news to know that when we become like Him in His death, we inherit the power of a warrior for the battles of our life.

Dostoyevsky said, "The terrible thing is that beauty is not only frightening but a mystery as well. That's where God and the devil join battle, and their battlefield is the heart of man."[14] Our hearts are indeed a battle-field, and the devil seeks to mar the beauty of God in us. But he cannot win. All God's beauty, all God's won-der, all God's power are ours because the warrior Jesus is ours! He is in us to win. And that is power worth dying for.

WALKING THE PATH OF DEADLY POWER

I must admit that I sometimes take the Lord's Supper for granted. It often seems to be a ritual that we repeat over and over without a lot of meaning associated. But that's not so in persecuted churches....

I'll never think of the Lord's Supper in the same way since that day in southeast Asia. Three of us had traveled there to meet secretly with believers and train them. We had moved several times to stay away from the authorities and finally ended up on a beach hours from anywhere. People came from all over the country, a few by car, most by bus or bike, to that remote area. About seventy of us met in a small room with no breeze at all. The heat was sweltering. Each of us would take turns teaching and then collapse somewhere to try to rest. We were dangerously close to heatstroke. But the believers ate it up. They couldn't get enough. It was so rare for them to be able to worship together like this.

As we finished, we shared the Lord's Supper together. It was not translated, but it didn't need to be. I watched in awe as the bread and the cup were served—and the people wept. They wept as they took the Lord's Supper. At first they wept with a poignant sadness. The Lord they suffered for understood them. He had suffered for them too.

Died for them. But as we finished, the tears turned to tears of joy. The people began to sing. I asked an interpreter what they were singing. He said, "They are singing songs of joy because they are free!" I don't know how long they sang. It was late in the night when the three of us left to collapse and sleep somewhere, but they sang on. We saw them as suffering, in chains, to be pitied, but I have never seen people so free. Free through the cross! Free through death.

Are you ready for that freedom? You can seek it in safe places, but you won't find it there. You will find it only on a deadly path.

MY DEAR FRIEND Gary Witherall's wife was murdered by a terrorist in Lebanon in 2002. I told Gary I was writing a book on authentic power and using Philippians 3:10 as my guide. Gary said, "That is a powerful verse, but no one will ever understand it until they are terrified." I found his statement strange at first, but as I thought about it, "becoming like him in his death" *is* a terrifying thing. But I am more terrified to miss it. There is power there. It is deadly power. But it is exactly what we need. And it's all we need.

So if you're ready, stop where you are and get alone.

Hit your knees, or even your face. Tell Him you are ready to count yourself dead. Empty yourself. Go through in your mind all the things you hold precious, all that you would like to keep for yourself, under your own control, and empty it before Him. Tell Him that, like Paul, you want to know His power and nothing will stop you. You are ready to become like Him in His death. And then you will die. And you will begin to know His deadly power.

And you will begin to really live. Because one thing is for sure.

When you die with Jesus, resurrection is on the way!

CHAPTER FOUR

ARRIVING AT THE REALM OF THE RESURRECTION

...and so, somehow, to attain to the resurrection from the dead.

PHILIPPIANS 3:11

Have courage for the great sorrows of life and patience for the small ones. And when you have finished your daily task, go to sleep in peace. God is awake.

VICTOR HUGO

God is awake.

And He calls us to awaken and be with Him—in all His power. It's the central message of the gospel. We've been on a journey together to get to this point. We began by opening a door—the doorway of the desperate. We walked through that door, gasping for God, longing to know Him and His resurrection power. To know Him by experience. But then we discovered that the road beyond that door was paved with pain. Yet you are still with me on the road. And we have stayed on this journey even as we have seen that the road leads to a deadly place. That we cannot bypass the cross to get to power. So much of this journey, because it has been a journey with Jesus, has been difficult and dark. But now we are about to emerge into the light. Into the light of lights. We have reached our destination—an empty tomb. We have arrived at the resurrection realm. And this was exactly what Paul was after.

Paul uses the word *attain,* meaning to arrive, to come directly to the destination, to touch. Some scholars have debated what Paul was saying here. Maybe he was talking about heaven and believed he had to work his way there. Or maybe he was referring to a mystical state of mind. I don't believe he meant either of these. Paul wanted to go to the tomb!

If Paul was going to be like Jesus in His death, he wanted to know what it was to walk out of the tomb with Jesus alive. He wanted the power of the resurrection. To feel the cold stone as he touched the walls of the crypt, to see the beauty of the sun as he stepped out with Jesus. To exhilarate in the first breath of resurrected life. Paul wanted it all. More than is humanly possible. He wanted authentic power—to live in the strength Jesus had as He came out of the tomb.

We must remember two things about authentic power. First, it is not a nostalgic remembering of the resurrection. It is bringing the power of the resurrection into real-time living. And second, it wasn't just for Paul. He told us as much. It is every believer's legacy: "If *we* have been united with him like this in his death, *we* will certainly also be united with him in his resurrection" (Romans 6:5). I love that word *certainly*. This is for all of us—*we*. And if we hear the word *resurrection* and think only of heaven, we miss the point. Read Romans 6 again. Does it sound like Paul is talking about life by and by? No! He's talking about life here and now. He's talking about authentic power:

**You have the ability to live every moment
in the same strength Jesus had as
He stepped out of the tomb.**

That's where we've arrived together. And it's a very good place to be. But it's also an easy place to miss. A place many believers walk right past on their way to lesser things.

Because the resurrection realm is a part of the invisible world, it can tend to seem less real. Of course, it is complete foolishness to think that *invisible* means nonexistent or less powerful, as my adventures with electricity continue to remind me. And the invisible realm of the resurrection is constantly invading the visible world of every believer. We just seem determined to miss it.

One evening, I had gone to pick up my son at the movie theater near our house. The movie wasn't out yet so I parked at the curb and waited. I saw a young man coming toward me. He tapped on my window, so I rolled it down a little and looked into a pair of very confused eyes. "Hey dude," he said, "could you possibly give me a ride to the movie theater?"

I looked deeply into his eyes for a moment, searching for a sign that any brain activity was actually taking place. Seeing none, I simply pointed to the theater entrance directly beside my car and said, "Buddy, you're in luck. You have arrived."

With complete shock he stared at the theater and uttered that glorious exclamation of suddenly discovered truth: "Dude!"

Maybe we're not much different. Stupefied by the narcotic affect of powerless religion in the visible world, we walk right by what we are really looking for. But God, in His patience and mercy, points us to His power. When we first see it, we have a choice. To say "Dude!" in our surprise at the power of God's resurrection realm and hold out hope that we wander into it again sometime, or to decide that what we see is so compelling and powerful that we will leave behind what clouds our vision and learn to live in this realm, in this power, every minute. That last one is the choice we should be after.

OUT OF THE TOMB WITH JESUS

As I write this, I am thinking about my next trip to Israel. I can't wait to go back to the Garden Tomb I wrote about in the introduction. I have a unique opportunity to film part of a message there, so I'll be taking a camera inside the tomb. I'll show people the place where Jesus lay. Then I'll show them the view He had as the stone rolled away and He first looked out into the resurrection morning air. And then I will invite all those watching to join me in their hearts as I take the first step out of the tomb–the same step Jesus took. I can't wait! I want those who hear the message to grasp this, as I want you to: *The very same power He had in that step is freely offered to us.* "For to be sure, he was crucified in weakness, yet he lives by God's power. Likewise, we are weak in him, yet by God's power we will live with him to serve you" (2 Corinthians 13:4).

The truth of that passage is so important to us. We are meant to be joined with Him. The power He had as He walked out of the tomb, the power He lives in right now, we are to live in. And Paul makes it clear that this power is meant to be used to serve now, not just in heaven.

So what is the nature of the power Jesus had as He stepped out of the tomb? As amazing as it sounds, that power is ours too.

THE POWER OF ETERNITY

The most basic fact of our faith is that Jesus Christ was physically raised from the dead. "Remember Jesus Christ, raised from the dead, descended from David. This is my gospel" (2 Timothy 2:8). The gospel has no good news if Jesus did not come out of that tomb.

As a part of my doctoral work, I studied for a semester at a seminary of another denomination. This denomination had lost half its membership in the last twenty years with no sign of the decline slowing. After my first day of class, it wasn't hard to see why. The course was a study of evangelical and liberal Christians in contemporary life. On the first day, the professor told us that belief in the resurrection of Christ was what defined someone as an evangelical, rather than a liberal. That certainly raised my eyebrows since it seems pretty clear that professing the resurrection is the beginning point of *any* Christian!

He then asked us to go around the circle and share our beliefs about the resurrection. I happened to be last. About ten people were in that circle, and it turned out that a grand total of *one* believed Jesus rose from the dead. Me! I couldn't believe it. These were seminary students training to be ministers. One guy said he believed something happened, but he didn't know what. The others seemed to find it almost humorous that people still believed in the resurrection. The last person to speak before me was a very angry woman. She proceeded to talk about the horrible fundamentalists and all the harm they had done to the world with their outdated beliefs. She was especially harsh about a particular Christian college near where she lived, Criswell College—which is where I was teaching at the time.

When it was my turn, I had so much fun that it was probably sinful. "I'm John Avant. I'm a pastor and a professor at Criswell College."

The woman beside me sank in her chair.

With a big smile I said, "This is the most wretched, pitiful group of people I have ever been in. And since you all seem very nice, I'm wondering if you know why I would say such a thing."

No one knew, not even the professor.

I said, "Well, because the Bible says so. First Corinthians 15 says if Christ is not raised, then everything you are doing here is futile. All your studies are a waste of time and you are the most wretched people in the world and worthy to be pitied more than anyone."

Faces were frozen. Jaws on the floor.

"And I'm just wondering, since all of you are studying for the ministry, and since for two thousand years billions of people have been so impressed by the evidence of the resurrection that they have given their life to this One they believe is alive, what evidence have you discovered that negates all that?"

There was dead silence. Then one young man blurted out, "Well, people just don't rise from the dead!"

"Unless they are God," I replied.

That was it. That was the entire argument from the group against the resurrection of Christ. I was stunned. I asked permission to present the evidence for the resurrection. No interest. I asked if anyone had ever even looked at the evidence. No interest.

The rest of the semester was pretty much a rambling discussion of leftist theologians searching for some obscure meaning in life apart from God. It was also a pointed reminder to me that there is no power at all without the resurrection. Those students were preparing to lead a dying life in dying churches in a dying denomination. I ended up so challenged by the experience that I did my doctoral dissertation on the effect of its loss of biblical truth on this denomination. It was a sad and staggering study.

The reason the resurrection is so critical is that it brings the power of eternity into daily life. Now, you may think I'm contradicting myself. I know I said that resurrection power is for *present-day* life. But if this life is *all* there is, then what's the motivation for it all anyway? If everything I do will end up as dust, and if everything all of us do will simply vanish one day, then why bother? But if it is true, if He did rise, and if we are united with Him, then the very power of eternity enters all we do now.

And that *is* the truth!

We don't have to wait for heaven for eternal power. God has initiated the power of eternity in us now. "And God raised us up with Christ and seated us with him in the heavenly realms in Christ Jesus" (Ephesians 2:6). We have the strength to do all God calls us to do in this life–even the impossible–because impossible power lives in us. We have the motivation to walk through suffering and even death as we follow Jesus because we know that what we do here matters forever. That's resurrection power–the power of eternity for this passing moment.

THE POWER OF HIS PERSONAL PRESENCE

Perhaps the hardest thing for me to understand about believers today is how many continue to view Christianity as "what we do at church on Sunday" rather than a vibrant, every-minute relationship with the risen Christ. We don't live in the Old Testament anymore. We don't go to the temple and stand far away from a God we are afraid of. We can come into the holy of holies and find God there, calling us in His love to know Him, to walk with Him in His power.

When Jesus stepped out of the tomb, the world changed. He told His disciples that He would never leave them, that He would be with them always. His resurrected body has no limits. He *is* the resurrection (John 11:25), so He doesn't send power to us; He becomes power in us.

But for many it's just easier to view Jesus as a compartmentalized segment of our lives. That way we don't have to give up our control—but we do give up our power. Winston Churchill said, "Men occasionally stumble over the truth, but most of them pick themselves up and hurry off as if nothing had happened." Don't run past the personal presence of Jesus. He died and rose to give it to you!

I love 2 Timothy 4:16–18. I think those verses are among the most tender and poignant in the Bible. Paul is in his last days and he knows it. He is on trial for his life. He says:

> At my first defense, no one came to my support, but everyone deserted me. May it not be held against them. But the Lord stood at my side and gave me strength, so that through me the message might be fully proclaimed and all the Gentiles might hear it. And I was delivered from the lion's mouth. The Lord will rescue me from every evil attack and will bring me safely to his heavenly kingdom. To him be glory for ever and ever. Amen.

Now that's personal power! What does it mean to step out of the tomb with Jesus? That when you are completely

alone, you will not be alone. That when you face the greatest challenges, struggles, losses, and fears of your life, He
will stand by your side. Just think about that for a
moment—the Creator of the universe, standing by your
side. When you are attacked by evil, you will not be
harmed. And when you die, you will never have been as
safe as at that moment. That's the personal power that
stepped out of the tomb and right to your side.

THE POWER OF SIGNIFICANCE

From the moment of Jesus' resurrection, everything began
to revolve around mission. The first person to see Him alive,
Mary Magdalene, was told to "go...and tell" (John 20:17).
She was the first missionary. And from that point forward,
everyone who chose to follow Him had a life on mission, a
life on purpose.

And the Great Commission extended that purpose to
all of us. But the resurrection does even more than give us
purpose. It gives us significance. Our purpose is not small.
It is the shared purpose of Jesus Himself. We can follow
Him anywhere to do anything on an adventure that matters and do it with perfect confidence that He is going not
only with us but just before us to chart the way.

When Jesus stepped out of the tomb, He stepped out on mission. And we are not sent *for* Him on *our* mission; we are sent *with* Him on *His* mission and behind Him as He leads. His promise of authentic power is His word to you that where you step today, He is stepping too. You can walk another direction if you wish, but why? As long as you walk with Him, you walk in the strength He brought with Him out of the tomb. You walk into guaranteed significance. It makes absolutely no difference how small or difficult your assignment may seem. You walk in resurrection significance now.

For a scuba diver, nothing is more exciting and mysterious than a wreck. I have been inside barges, airplanes, German World War II ships, and a Russian destroyer, all far beneath the surface. I recently read an amazing book called *Shadow Divers* about the discovery of a previously unknown German submarine in the Atlantic Ocean. The sub was so deep that a man could easily die on the dive, and several have. The most terrifying thing for a wreck diver is to go into a section of a deep wreck never explored before. And yet that was the challenge these divers faced:

It is one thing, wreck divers will tell you, to slither in near-total darkness through a shipwreck's twisted, broken mazes, each room a potential trap of swirling silt and collapsing structure. It is another to do so without knowing that someone did it before you and lived.[15]

What a relief that *we* never have to make that dive! We'll have all the adventure we can handle in this life, but we never have to go anywhere He is not. He is on mission with us and leads us into the dark, into the wreckage of this world. And with Him are light and hope and strength. Knowing that your purpose is important, and that it is empowered by the resurrection, makes it significant! Empowered purpose. That's what Jesus came out of the tomb with—and that's what you have too.

THE POWER TO CONQUER

In the last chapter we saw that the death of Christ gives you the power of a warrior. That's good, but the power to conquer is even better. A warrior can be defeated, but by definition a conqueror wins. Every time. And when Jesus came out of the tomb, He came out as the Conqueror who cannot be defeated. Ephesians 1:20 tells us the mighty strength of the resurrection. Verses 21–22 reveal the result of that strength. Jesus is now "far above all rule and authority, power and dominion, and every title that can be given, not only in the present age but also in the one to come. And God placed all things under his feet."

All things! Think about that. He is the winner. There is no competition. Everything that could come against Him, He now stands on top of. They are under His feet. And if you step out of the tomb with Him, then you stand where He stands—on top of all that. There is no more need to fear. For the rest of your life, whatever you face, you only need to remember this—He wins, so you win!

I took two good friends to see the movie *The Passion of the Christ*. Both had been spiritual seekers, and I had just helped the wife to receive Christ. As we watched that amazing movie, we came to my favorite part—the resurrection. The scene lasts only a few seconds but is incredible in its impact. As Jesus sits up in the tomb, the camera shows his face—not a face of blissful happiness, but of determined mission. And then as war drums beat out a call to battle, Jesus stands up and steps out of the tomb. I wanted to jump and shout when I saw this, but something better happened. My friend, a brand-new follower of Christ, said, "Now I understand. Jesus is a warrior!"

Yes! And a conquering warrior at that. And as He

conquers, so do we. We step with Him into every victory we will ever need, today, tomorrow, forever.

That's authentic power. That's life in the resurrection realm. Now I want to ask you this: If you could step out of the tomb, rise with Christ, live forever, with an eternal motivation, with empowered significance, taking every step knowing that Jesus is with you and before you, and be guaranteed to win, what would you do to get that life?

The good news is that it is already done.

POWER FAITH

Paul said he wanted to *somehow* attain to the resurrection (v. 11). He didn't know any way to get there *on his own*. Neither do I. The way to resurrection power is the same way to knowing Christ—by faith. The faith you need is not faith to get something you don't have but rather faith to believe in what you do have.

Many years ago, George Whitefield wrote that "the power of his resurrection is as great now as formerly." Do you believe that? Or have you slowly slipped into an unspoken faithlessness that leaves spiritual power within the pages of the Bible—real, but only in ancient history? You have to decide. Will you choose to believe that resurrection power is waiting for you, already given as a gift, as real as the first Easter morning? That belief is power faith, and without it you will never know authentic power. Because all of God's promises, including His promise of power, are received by faith. There is no other way.

Which is very good news! It means that nothing is keeping you from Christ's power! You don't need more money, a better job, or your problems solved. You don't need to be smarter or have a better plan. You just need to want Him. To long for His power like Paul did. A. W. Tozer said:

> I want deliberately to encourage this mighty longing after God. The lack of it has brought us to our present low estate. The stiff and wooden quality about our religious lives is a result of our lack of holy desire. Complacency is a deadly foe of all spiritual growth. Acute desire must be present or there will be no manifestation of Christ to His people. He waits to be wanted. Too bad that with many of us He waits so long, so very long, in vain.[16]

He waits to be wanted!

Is He waiting for you? He's waited long enough. Ask

Him by faith, right now, to begin to manifest His power in and through your life, to unleash His Spirit who is already within you in ways that can be explained only by His power. Trust Him. Believe that He will do it as surely as He died and rose again to save you. Pray the prayer of Amy Carmichael from so long ago: "Make me thy fuel, flame of God!" By the promise of God, your life will become the wood in which the fire of His power burns.

"Where's the power of the resurrection?" Gary asked. Let's go eat some more Indian food and talk. Because it's been here all along. We just haven't really wanted it. But it's waiting for us, just like it was for Paul. Now that we've learned how to recognize resurrection power, the next question is: How are we to *live* in resurrection power?

PART TWO:

THE ROAD MAP THROUGH THE RESURRECTION REALM

The greatest danger facing all of us...is not that we shall make an absolute failure of life, nor that we shall fall into outright viciousness, nor that we shall be terribly unhappy, nor that we shall feel life has no meaning at all—not these things. The danger is that we may fail to perceive life's greatest meaning, fall short of its highest good, miss its deepest and most abiding happiness, be unable to tender the most needed service, be unconscious of life ablaze with the Presence of God—and be content to have it so—that is the danger: that someday we may wake up and find that always we have been busy with husks and trappings of life and have really missed life itself.

PHILLIP BROOKS, 1835–1893

CHAPTER FIVE

THE GIANT JOURNEY INTO SMALLNESS

Not that I have already obtained all this, or have already been made perfect...

PHILIPPIANS 3:12

I knew God was looking for a man little enough that He could show Himself strong through him.

MISSIONARY HUDSON TAYLOR,
ON THE SECRET OF HIS SUCCESS

I am a lover of the journey. Always have been.

When I flew in an airplane for the first time at age eighteen, I couldn't understand why everyone around me seemed so calm and detached. We were flying! I had never felt so alive.

Even now I sense the wonder every time I fly. Since that first experience, my journeys have been many and amazing. I have climbed mountains, hiked through jungles, plunged beneath the sea. I have seen beautiful countries, dangerous countries, paradise lands, and poverty-stricken wastelands.

I have never tired of the new—a new country, a new friend, a new experience. And many of my new experiences have provided lasting (and occasionally painful) memories. Several years ago, I was speaking in Canada and was invited to go skiing. I couldn't wait. This was one sport I had always wanted to try. Most of the group I was with had been skiing for a long time. They just hopped on the lift and took off for the high slopes.

I, on the other hand, was sent to a class on the bunny hill—with ten six-year-olds. I listened to the instructor for a few minutes and then gave it a try. No problem at all. This was easy! Down the gentle slope I went, relishing the cold breeze against my face. Wow! I was a natural!

The instructor called our group of grade-schoolers and me together for a second lesson. I was having none of this. I had water-skied for many years, which had obviously equipped me with all the skills I needed, so I slipped away from the first-graders and hopped on the lift. What a gorgeous view! I figured the best plan was to go all the way to the top so I'd have more time to show off my new skills as I zipped down the mountain. Besides, "black diamond" sounded like a really cool name for a ski trail.

Off I went! As I crested the top of the hill, I realized that I was headed down—straight down. This was all right, though, because fast is fun. So I did what I had seen the Olympic guys do. I tucked down into a squat and flew! A small problem—a very sharp curve—loomed up ahead. It was at that point that I began to experience that uh-oh feeling I know so well. While the kiddies were at the bottom of the hill learning how to turn, I was leaving the trail, airborne, and heading straight for the trees.

Somewhere in the forest ahead of me I thought I heard the lovely voice of Sonny Bono singing, "I got you, babe!" Fortunately, I hit branches instead of trunks and hit my hand rather than my head. As I dug myself out from the snow, I thought, *Is my thumb supposed to bend in that direction?* One of these days I'll have the surgery to correct the damage, but for now I am regularly reminded that some journeys can be dangerous. And the more exciting the journey, the more painful the results can be. Giant journeys can be even bigger disasters.

No journey is more crucial, more exciting, and more dangerous than the journey into the resurrection realm, where we find the promise of God's authentic power. And the strange truth is that the only way to ski these advanced slopes successfully is to master the ability to turn in the right direction. And the right direction is the small path.

The journey into authentic power is a giant journey into smallness.

SMALL GIANTS OF THE MISSION FIELD

The restaurant where I was eating was a thousand years old. I've eaten at a few places where the food tasted that old, but the food here was great. And they really had been serving it for a thousand years.

I was in one of the oldest cities in the world, and everything around me was exotic. The rich aroma of the feast before me. The sounds of the nearby marketplace. The music. The clothes. Everything seemed strange, but I was the stranger here. During our visit to this city, the only other Americans we had seen were the family we came to visit. We sat eating together with them, a man, his wife, and their children—all eight of them. How they had come to be here was an amazing story.

This was a second marriage for both of them. Their first marriages had been spent on the mission field, where both had lost their spouses to illnesses. Each was left alone with four children. Later they met, fell in love, married, and returned to the country where we were eating—sort of the *Brady Bunch* of missions. I found myself working hard not to stare at them. *They are not normal,* I thought. Normal people don't respond to tragedy as they have. Normal people get angry with God and abandon Him because He didn't make their life easy. Normal people figure that God had His shot to take care of them on the mission field and didn't come through. Normal people don't just pack up their new marriage and eight kids and head into danger and uncertainty—again. No, they're not normal. Sitting with them, *I* felt very normal, but I also felt a strange envy. I wanted to be "not normal" too.

As we walked down the street together after lunch, the husband said to me, "You know, John, today is the anniversary of my first wife's death."

I could hardly believe it.

"I have cried and questioned and hurt so much over her death," he said. "But here in this place, on this mission that God has called our family to, I feel alive and in the middle of God's plan."

Not normal. Wonderfully so.

Sitting here writing these words in my very comfortable and semi-normal world, I am struck by several things: No one where they live even knows they are missionaries.

Almost no one in America knows where they serve. What if God does a mighty work through them? What if a movement begins there that sweeps across the region and changes history? What if they are successful beyond their wildest dreams? *No one will know it was them.* They won't hear applause. They won't be famous. They will quietly watch the power of God at work.

And that's the point. It is the power of *God* we are talking about. It is not ours. God's power can never be *mine*. It is always wholly His. It cannot be co-opted, achieved, or owned. It is His. He loves to display it through you though. To baptize you in it, to fill you with it. But He'll do it only if you are willing to be small. To be unknown, that He might be known. To be small, that He might be big. Like this wonderful, abnormal, beautiful family who will tuck in their eight children in their three bedrooms on the other side of the world tonight—these small giants of the mission field.

MY CALL TO BE SMALL

Paul struggled to be small. You can see it so often in his writings. He was tempted to brag and sometimes gave in to the temptation. He was a man who knew how to live in God's power and yet was drawn to his own. How important was it to God to keep Paul small? So important that He allowed a demon to torment Paul to do it.

Many people are familiar with Paul's "thorn in the flesh," but don't know what it was or why he had it. The Bible answers both questions: "To keep me from becoming conceited because of these surpassingly great revelations, there was given me a thorn in my flesh, a messenger of Satan, to torment me" (2 Corinthians 12:7). The word *messenger* also means *angel*. God allowed an angel of Satan, a demon, to have limited ability to oppress Paul so that he would be forced to depend on God. God loved Paul too much to allow him to drift into pride. God fought for Paul! And Paul himself said that this thorn was the secret to the power of God in his life: "Therefore I will boast all the more gladly about my weaknesses, so that Christ's power may rest on me" (v. 9).

If God hadn't pressed Paul into smallness like this, he might have missed authentic power altogether. It was about seven years later when Paul wrote the passage from Philippians that this book is based on. He was obviously smaller by then. The thorn had done its work. He was in full pursuit of all God's power but had no illusions that he had caught it all. "Not that I have already obtained all this…" (Philippians 3:12). The word *obtained* means "to understand fully." The tense Paul used indicates that he didn't get all he was after in one experience. In the next phrase, "or have already been made perfect" (v. 12), he uses a different Greek tense to show that he still had not achieved it all. Paul was far down the road to smallness now—right in the place where God could use him in big ways.

I have always thought big is better. When I was a pastor, my goal was to preach to a bigger crowd, to see more people come to Christ and more people join our church. These are not bad goals in themselves, but it is easy for them to become signs that I am big rather than opportunities to bring glory and honor to God. If we get bigger through our own efforts and plans, then we will have a building with lots of people in it and nothing more. God values smallness, blesses smallness, and uses smallness in giant ways. The theme of smallness is very big in the Bible! When God sent His Son to this world for us, He chose a small place for His birth:

> "But you, Bethlehem Ephrathah, though you are small among the clans of Judah, out of you will come for me one who will be ruler over Israel, whose origins are from old, from ancient times." (Micah 5:2)

Jesus grew up in a *small* town with a *small* family and a *small* job. Everything about His life modeled humility. He taught that smallness did not hinder the power of God at all. "If you have faith as *small* as a mustard seed, you can say to this mulberry tree, 'Be uprooted and planted in the sea,' and it will obey you" (Luke 17:6). And using the same tiny seed as an illustration, Jesus made one of the most amazing statements of His ministry:

> "What shall we say the kingdom of God is like, or what parable shall we use to describe it? It is like a mustard seed, which is the *smallest* seed you plant in the ground. Yet when planted, it grows and becomes the largest of all garden plants, with such big branches that the birds of the air can perch in its shade." (Mark 4:30–32)

Jesus says that His entire reign, His kingdom, must begin small wherever it grows. Jesus is not looking for people with big enough talents to use, but people with small enough ambition, ego, and self-interest in whom He can plant the seed of His kingdom, which will grow so far beyond us that we will be lost in its shade—and filled with His power!

The most prevalent word I have heard from God for my own life in recent months is *small*. When I am alone with Him, I sense it often. I hear His call to smallness and His gentle rebuke of my longing for recognition and success.

Helen Keller said, "I long to accomplish great and noble tasks, but it is my chief duty to accomplish humble tasks as though they were great and noble." My *chief duty*! This is exactly what Jesus teaches, but it is so hard for me. I am drawn to the big and visible assignments. I have had the privilege of speaking to thousands of people every week, but lately I have begun to sense from God that He is not measuring my life by how many I speak to or how well I speak. I sense that He is more interested in whether I have time for one person. One person who is lonely, who is lost, who thinks I'm too busy for him or that everyone is too busy for him.

I love to preach. I know that God has called me to it. But I keep hearing God say, "Be small, John. Talk to a child. Pray with a widow. Counsel a wounded heart. Slow down. Follow Me."

I am constantly aware of how far from the fullness of God's power I am. Yet it is not because I am not big enough, but because I so often refuse to be small enough. The paradoxical but practical guide to power in my life these days is this:

God allows me to experience the greatest power in the places where I am noticed the least.

In these places *He* can be big. His power can be unleashed, unhindered by my pitiful imitations. This is the giant journey into smallness I so want to be on.

THE DECEPTIVE DANGER OF GETTING LARGER

All my life I have struggled to keep my weight under control. I have done better in recent years because I run a lot, but oh, how I love to eat! My doctor reminds me that it is important that I stay in shape since my blood pressure is marginal. Of course, high blood pressure is known as the silent killer because it has no symptoms. *And* overeating is one of its chief causes. You can get larger and larger and feel fine, but be in terrible health.

In the ancient world and in other eras, people believed that being fat was a sign of health and prosperity. It may well be that we have not yet learned our lesson. In the Western church, we have many large churches, plenty of money, and even national influence, as evangelicals are widely credited with the election of President Bush. But we are in terrible danger of being large, but also sick and power-less without even knowing it. Author Jerry White says,

"No one is so empty as the man who has stopped walking with God and doesn't know it." The same can be said of churches and even nations.

If Christians are to embrace smallness, we must first recognize how our pride and self-absorbed largeness have blinded us to our need and robbed us of God's power. Proverbs 11:2 tells us that "when pride comes, then comes disgrace, but with humility comes wisdom." That's pretty clear. Choose to enlarge ourselves and we become a disgrace. Choose to humbly pursue the largeness of God and we become wise. In the New Testament, Peter tells us that there is absolutely no way we can live in anything resembling authentic power if we try to do so in our own pride, because God Himself will become our opponent: "God opposes the proud but gives grace to the humble" (1 Peter 5:5). To be sure we get it, James tells us the same thing, word for word (James 4:6).

This is why all the power of the enemy is aligned against you at this very moment—to keep you from even considering repentance, brokenness, humility, and smallness as options. In C. S. Lewis's *The Screwtape Letters,* Satan instructs one of his demons with the following warning:

I see only one thing to do at the moment. Your patient has become humble; have you drawn his attention to the fact? All virtues are less formidable to us once the man is aware that he has them, but this is specially true of humility. Catch him at the moment when he is really poor in spirit and smuggle into his mind the gratifying reflection, "By Jove! I'm being humble," and almost immediately pride at his own humility will appear.[17]

There is our battle if we are to live in the resurrection realm of real power. Before we look at how to actually live a life of smallness, let's look at the very large gifts that come to small people.

THE BIG GIFTS OF SMALLNESS

There is an obvious danger in asking what we get for being small. We risk seeking largeness for ourselves. It is a tremendous challenge for us in our natural self-centeredness to focus wholly on God, His glory, His largeness. But the truth is that there are tremendous advantages to choosing the small road. It *is* the giant journey. It is where Christ's resurrection power can be found. And the road that takes you there is paved with some wonderful gifts.

THE SMELL OF JESUS

Almost every Christmas, I buy my wife perfume. It always seems interesting to me that the most expensive kinds are generally the ones in the smallest bottles. The big gallon-size bucket for $19.95, which I'd choose, is usually not the one that will impress my sweet wife. Our smallness smells sweet to God. One of the most interesting passages of the Bible tells us that all believers have a spiritual aroma. We are meant to smell like Jesus:

> But thanks be to God, who always leads us in triumphal procession in Christ and through us spreads everywhere the fragrance of the knowledge of him. For we are to God the aroma of Christ among those who are being saved and those who are perishing. (2 Corinthians 2:14–15)

This is what we are *to God*!

When we choose the small road of humility, servanthood, and selflessness, we become valuable to God and to the world—like that small bottle of fine perfume. We smell like Jesus. When we work hard in our own way, in our own strength, we may get larger, but we are only producing our own spiritual sweat. And no one wants to smell a giant jar of my sweat. How would you feel if you knew that when you come into a room, people feel like the whole atmosphere has grown sweeter, like the aroma of Jesus has entered with you? That's a wonderful gift to find along the small road.

THE WONDER OF LIFE

The great evangelist Gypsy Smith said late in his life, "I have never lost the wonder." I am convinced that the church is in desperate need of the restoration of wonder. When I was a pastor, I was constantly challenged by the task of leading people to live as if Jesus is real. Most believers are so overwhelmed by the stuff of today that they are lulled into thinking that life is dull. What a tragedy! We think that if we can accomplish enough impressive things, sooner or later we will surely impress ourselves—and God. But the One who created the universe is not very impressed with any of our efforts. We are in danger of becoming like the people of whom Coach Barry Switzer said: "Some people are born on third base and go through life thinking they hit a triple." All we have is from God anyway!

If we want to be really impressed, to live in wonder

and awe, we *must* find it on the small road—where we constantly watch the big things God is doing, rather than obsessing about ourselves (except for a few hours on Sunday). We need what I call *empowered dissatisfaction*. Just glimpses of God's authentic power will cause us to be dissatisfied with anything less. We will return to wonder, and we will keep growing, learning, and moving close to the edge of our seats. I love what Frederick Buechner says in his book *The Hungering Dark*:

> Those who believe in God can never in a way be sure of Him again. Once they have seen him in a stable, they can never be sure where he will appear or to what lengths he will go or to what ludicrous depths of self-humiliation he will descend in his wild pursuit of man.[18]

That's the wonder we need to recover! And it's found on the small road.

A UNIVERSAL OPPORTUNITY

The simple fact of the matter is that not all people can be big. Most will not be the CEO, the number one draft pick, the valedictorian, or the Oscar winner. If your goal is to be big, you are almost guaranteed to live a disappointing life. Even if you get big, very few *stay* big. There is always a new star athlete, a new business leader, the new face of the moment. *But everyone can be small.*

Jesus was always more impressed by small people than big ones. In Luke 21, Jesus watched rich people give their offerings, but was impressed only by a woman who gave two copper coins: "This poor widow has put in more than all the others. All these people gave their gifts out of their wealth; but she out of her poverty put in all she had to live on" (vv. 3–4). Not everyone can be rich, but everyone can be sacrificial. Like a poor widow two thousand years ago, you could be remembered for all of history. Not for your "big" accomplishments, but for your pursuit of smallness. That's a gift available to everyone.

PRACTICAL POWER

To the average person, spiritual power often sounds like something mystical and hard to define—not anything that is helpful in daily life. But I've found evidence to the contrary in a surprising source—*Good to Great,* a bestselling business book by Jim Collins. It is the only book of its kind that I have asked our entire staff to read.

Collins led an empirical study of companies that had

gone from being good companies to great companies and had sustained it for at least fifteen years. The most crucial finding of the study is that all good-to-great companies had what Collins calls *level five leaders*. These leaders were exactly the opposite of what the world would expect a hard-driving successful CEO to look like. "The good-to-great leaders never wanted to become larger-than-life heroes."[19] In other words, they had chosen to be small. Collins says that "level five leaders display a compelling modesty, are self-effacing and understated."[20] They embody a "paradoxical mix of personal humility and professional will."[21] They were committed to excellence in their business, but not for their own sake. They dedicated themselves to the success of their company, not themselves.

I had the opportunity to spend some time with Collins at a conference recently. I mentioned that I thought his book was the best business book I had ever read. He told me, "*Good to Great* is not a business book. It is a *life* book."

So there we are. Empirical evidence that biblical humility is the only road to the kind of leadership that is practical and effective. This is not church stuff we're talking about. This is real-life power that makes a difference in everything we do and is found only on the small road.

REAL SUCCESS

The truly wonderful thing about choosing smallness is that we are no longer dependent on our own pitiful efforts to be a success. We have joined ourselves to the success of Another. Even if we appear to fail in the eyes of everyone around us, our ultimate success is not compromised. Tozer summarized the giant journey to smallness so well:

> Our great honor lies in being just what Jesus was and is. To be accepted by those who accept Him, rejected by all who reject Him, loved by those who love Him and hated by everyone that hates Him. What greater glory could come to any man?
>
> We can afford to follow Him to failure. Faith dares to fail. The resurrection and the judgment will demonstrate before all worlds who won and who lost. We can wait.[22]

That is real success! God's authentic power is so big
that staying small is simply a matter of keeping this amazing truth right before our eyes and our heart: We have
been rescued by the cross. We have come out of the tomb
with Jesus. We can live every moment in that awesome
power. And with that in mind, we should be small enough
to continue our journey into the resurrection realm of
authentic power.

CHAPTER SIX

THE PURPOSE PURSUING LIFE

...but I press on to take hold of that for which Christ Jesus took hold of me.

PHILIPPIANS 3:12

Moses spent forty years thinking he was
   somebody,
forty years learning he was nobody, and
forty years discovering what God can do
with a nobody.

D. L. MOODY

We are works in progress! But we don't have 120 years to learn how to live in God's power—we're going to have to improve on Moses' record. The need for God's authentic power in our lives is so real, so urgent, that we have no time to waste at all. We need to go after it today!

I'm forty-four years old. A few months ago, I got the crazy idea that I wanted to get in the best shape of my life and weigh the same as I did on my wedding day—when I was twenty. So I began four months of training to run a half-marathon, 13.1 miles. I had stumbled through this race twice before, but this time I was determined to get in serious shape, to shatter my personal record, and to look like a twenty-year-old again.

I was seriously committed. I ate like a rabbit and ran until I dropped. And I reached my goal! I lost almost thirty pounds and ran the race with ease, twenty-one minutes *faster* than my previous time. On Thanksgiving Day 2004, I weighed what I did on my wedding day. And so, in full-blown midlife crisis mode, I stood in front of the mirror barely clothed to admire my finely sculpted, twenty-year-old-like body (pathetic, I know, but just bear with me a moment).

As I stood gazing in the mirror, I realized, to my deep dismay, that something was amiss. Why after losing all that weight did I still have this little roll around my waist? I didn't have that when I was twenty. Why was all my remaining body fat relocating to this one spot? And what was this loose skin hanging under my chin? And why did just about every muscle in my body ache?

And why was a little of my hair no longer blond, but actually kind of…gray? And worst of all, why was there almost as much hair in my ears as on my head? I was a work in progress all right—progressing straight toward the nursing home!

I know this is the lot of us all, but what if we could reverse it? What if we could become stronger, *more* full of life, *more* powerful as we aged? We can! No, I'm not selling Avant's Magic Anti-Aging Cream or anything like that. Our bodies *are* going downhill, and only heaven will reverse that. But there is something wonderful God wants to do in our spirits—in the part of us that is really *us*. God wants our spirits to soar higher and stronger as we get older—to grow in strength until we are filled beyond belief with His awesome power. More and more. Day after day. Neverending. Who wouldn't go after that? The truth is, most don't. But all of us can.

A PURSUIT, NOT AN ARRIVAL

It's interesting that in all of Paul's talk about resurrection power, he never says that he *got* it. "But I press on," he says. He was after it, chasing it, but not ever catching it. He was pursuing, not arriving. The Greek word for *press on* means to chase, to "run swiftly as if to catch something," to pursue. It's a strong word used for athletes determined to win their race and hunters determined to catch their prey. Paul was in the race and on the hunt for "that for which Christ Jesus took hold of me."

That's an unusual statement, isn't it? I looked at over a dozen commentaries on this passage and found almost nothing about this phrase. What does it mean? Well, Paul says here that there is a reason Christ took hold of him—a purpose. He wanted to know all of it. He wanted to grasp all of the purpose of his life. We have already seen Paul's desperate desire to know resurrection power. Now we see his longing to know God's purpose. I believe that these two desires, when merged into one mighty longing, become the heart-cry of a Christ-follower for everything really needed in life. It is *empowered purpose* we are after! We want to know why we are on this earth and we want the power to live out that purpose. That *is* the promise of God's authentic power!

I was talking to my friend Johnny Hunt, pastor of First Baptist Church of Woodstock, Georgia, about this passage. He said, "When I read these words, I can almost feel His hand holding strong to my arm, as I hold strong to His, just when I need Him the most." Beautiful.

Empowered purpose to grip our life as we grip His. This is worth *taking hold* of. And when Paul says that he is after it, he is saying a lot. Taking hold of Christ and His purpose and being taken hold of by Him is the very essence of power. The Greek word translated *take hold of* is used in a few different ways that give a vivid picture of what this life of empowered purpose is like.

In Acts 4:13, the Sanhedrin *realized,* or took hold of, the fact that Peter and John were filled with courage, authority, and power not because of their education or position but because "they had been with Jesus." The Sanhedrin were "astonished" by this. A life of empowered purpose cannot be ignored by the world. It confronts and requires decision. That life must be *taken hold of*, either to push it away or embrace it. That life is the answer to the prayer of martyred missionary Jim Elliot: "Lord, make me a crisis man. Let me not be a milepost on a single road, but make me a fork that men must turn one way or another in facing Christ in me."

The life of empowered purpose is a possessed life. It has been given away and taken hold of by Another. In Mark 9:18, the word *take hold of* is translated *seizes* and is used of demon possession. Who or what do we want to control our purpose? When we are seized by God's

Spirit, we give control of our life to Him. What you take hold of determines what will *have* hold of you!

The life of empowered purpose is a pursuit, not an arrival. It is the embracing of mystery and wonder. In Ephesians 3:18, Paul uses the word *grasp* for "to take hold of." He prays that we will be able to grasp the fullness of God's love but then immediately says it can't be fully grasped. It does appear that the God who takes hold of us and calls us to take hold of Him and His purpose for us will not allow Himself to be fully caught. Why is this? Would it not seem that God would want us to catch Him, to *arrive?* In the Western church, we want to achieve, to finish, to accomplish our tasks. But this is not the way with God. Taking hold of Him is a journey.

THE PURPOSE DRIVEN LIFE AS JOURNEY

Rick Warren has given the church a priceless gift with his book *The Purpose Driven Life*. It has been a treasure of life wisdom for our church and for thousands of others. But I have been concerned recently to hear a growing number of people, particularly younger people with a postmodern perspective, express a kind of apathy or even dislike of the book. That surprised me, and I have since questioned

many about why they feel this way. The answers have all
been similar:

- "I don't want to systematize my life."
- "I don't think life fits in neat categories like that."
- "My life will never boil down to something as
  simple as a list of purposes."
- "This all sounds like something from the dead
  church where I grew up. It's for my parents, not
  for me."

There might be some validity to these charges if the
goal were to *arrive* at the final destination of our purposes
in life. If people think that, they've misinterpreted the
book. I like the book's title. God's empowered purpose
should drive my life. But it might help to think about the
book in terms of the journey. If we are not arriving, but
continually pursuing God's purposes for us, then our lives
become fluid, a narrative adventure—a purpose driven but
also *purpose pursuing* life!

Now, I don't want anyone to misunderstand me. I'm
not talking about a life with no absolutes, no foundational
truth to build upon. You don't have to give up truth in
order to be on a journey of purposeful pursuit. In fact, I

am deeply concerned that there are some evangelicals who openly call for a rejection of foundational truth. My friend Brian McClaren and I are dialoguing about this. His book *A New Kind of Christian* resulted in many labeling him as the theologian of the emerging church. His most recent book, *A Generous Orthodoxy,* more clearly spells out his theology.

Much about McClaren's writing resonates with and challenges me. He diagnoses many of the ills of the modern church accurately. However, I fear that his prescription could kill the patient. I would like to be wrong about this. Brian is one of the kindest men I have ever met. He has a genuine love for God and desire to see people come to Christ. I have told him that I appreciate so much about him that I hate to be his critic. But it seems to me that he is not really describing a new kind of Christian, but an old one—a repackaged neoorthodoxy that wants to embrace the beauty and general message of the Bible, while rejecting it as unchanging truth.

Perhaps what troubles me most about McClaren's writing is his assertion in *A Generous Orthodoxy* that "our *message* [my emphasis] and methodology have changed, do change, and must change."[23] This is not a typo or a slip by McClaren. He even spells it out on a chart. He believes that we must change our message. He goes so far as to question whether such things as the substitutionary atonement and the bodily resurrection of Christ are really fundamental to our faith. He rejects any form of foundationalism.

Maybe it surprises you that Brian and I are developing a friendship. It shouldn't. We need to be able to talk to each other and love each other even when we disagree. I pray that God fills Brian and others who share his views with all His authentic power. And if I have misrepresented Brian's views in any way, I hope he will forgive me, and I am ready to be corrected. But I also would like to convince these same friends that these teachings are not the answer. And that they are unnecessary. But they are not surprising.

Those who hold to these views are responding to the deadness and the tradition-imprisoned condition of so many churches, which appear to make the goal of the Christian journey to fit our lives into a stiff, wooden, religious system. But this is not the gospel. The answer to the state of the church today is not to abandon truth but to *journey into it*. I believe that this journey is the "new kind of Christian" God is really calling us to be. Not bound by irrelevant traditions and not rejecting the unchanging truths of God's Word, but pressing forward in community into the adventure of authentic power.

And there is no greater adventure, no wilder joy, no more liberating freedom than to agree with God that His Word speaks absolute truth and then to also agree with Him that we have not arrived at the destination of under-standing or experiencing it all. We are pursuing. We are pressing deeper. We want to know more of the mystery, the intricacies, the infinity of His purposes and His power. We want to *know* more of what we know. And to know more of what we don't yet know.

That is the journey! It is not a journey *away* from God's truth, but a journey deep *into* His truth.

I believe that anyone who honestly reads the Bible will come to the conclusion that the five purposes of our life that Warren identifies in his book are right on target. How can we approach them so that we stay small and embark on a journey into the largeness of God rather than seeing ourselves as having arrived? How would the *purpose dri-ven, purpose pursuing life* look different if we really began to live it? I believe the answers to these questions can plunge us into the sea of God's resurrection power.

EMPOWERING THE FIVE PURPOSES

I think it would help us to look at *worship, fellowship, discipleship, ministry,* and *evangelism,* the five purposes of the church that Warren discusses in *The Purpose Driven Life,* as if we were considering them for the first time. What would these concepts mean to us if we were on a new journey into them? What if we were new followers of Christ with no previous traditions or experience to influence us? I asked two of my good friends to do just that.

I call Bob and Marie my weird and wonderful friends. And they don't even mind! They are new Christ-followers and have virtually nothing in common with most churched Christians I know. But they do love Jesus. And they are on the journey to know Him more. I sat down with them for a few hours recently and asked them to share with me their thoughts on the five purposes of life. Their answers were fascinating. As we look at each of the purposes and think about how they might be lived out differently in a purpose pursuing life, I'll weave in some of Bob and Marie's thoughts. But first, you need to know their story.

I met Marie when she was a server at a restaurant where I was eating. She was from the Czech Republic and had only been in America a short time. I asked if I could pray for her as we blessed our food, and that opened up a wonderful discussion about her spiritual beliefs, which were highly New Age. I had the opportunity to pray for her and talk to her many times after that, and then one day she was gone. I later learned that she had returned to the Czech Republic. Almost two years passed, and one day she showed up at my office door. An old friend from America had come to visit her. They had fallen in love and had returned to America to be married. And they wanted me to do the wedding. I agreed, on the condition that they come to counseling with me.

When I met Marie's fiancé, Bob, I immediately liked him. We had a great discussion during which he told me in no uncertain terms that he was an atheist. This was going to be interesting. I had never married an atheist to a semi-Buddhist–New Ager before! Our counseling sessions continued and our friendship grew. But as their wedding day approached, neither Bob nor Marie was ready to accept Christ. Though I loved them, I wanted to be honest with them. I told them I would be leading them to make vows to the true God, in the Name of His Son, Jesus. I didn't want them to lie to God.

When I arrived for the wedding, I was immediately asked to go talk to Marie, who was upset about something.

When I walked into the bridal room, she said, "John, I don't want to lie to God! I need to call Him by name today. Please help me to accept Jesus into my life now!" For the first time in my life, I led a woman to Christ in her wedding dress. Bob married a brand-new follower of Christ that day.

After the wedding, my friendship with Bob really began to grow. One day, over lunch, we discovered that our political views were identical. That surprised me. I had Bob pegged for a liberal. But I was having lunch with a conservative, Republican atheist. Who was my really good friend. I asked Bob a question that day: "As a conservative who believes in absolute values, how can you be an atheist? Who do you think determined what the absolutes are?"

It was a turning point in his life. At our next lunch, Bob shocked me. "I am no longer an atheist!" he said. "You're right. There has to be a God who determines absolutes. But I have no idea who He is."

A few days later I showed him who God is. I took Bob and Marie to see *The Passion of the Christ*. It was a powerfully emotional time. Neither of them had much church background. They were very skeptical of the Bible. They knew little to nothing of the story they were watching.

And it captivated their hearts.

I have already told you of Marie's response. "Jesus is a warrior!" Not much later, Bob told me that the Jesus who did what he saw in the movie, the Jesus I had been telling him about, that was who God is. Bob the atheist became Bob the Christ-follower, and he would tell you himself that it still kind of freaks him out. Both he and Marie are still adjusting to a total change in their world-views. Over this first year of their new faith, it has sometimes been messy. But I love my weird and wonder-ful friends, and I love sharing their journey. I think it may help all of us to think through our own pursuit of the five empowered purposes of our lives.

WORSHIP

How would worship be different if it were viewed as a pursuit rather than an arrival? I believe we would find that most of the ways we think and talk about worship would be completely altered. How many times have you heard someone say after church, "The worship was really good today"? What does that mean? That the music was done well and according to my tastes? Or that the service made me feel good? Or, at best, that I really felt able to thank God for His goodness to me? These answers are flawed. They reflect an arrival mentality that says, "We achieved it. Our needs were met. Our goals were accomplished. Now on to the next thing."

But worship as pursuit is different. It's about the mystery and glory of God. It is *knowing God for God's own sake*. It shouldn't leave us commenting on how "good it was" or how "good we felt"—the ideal worship service should leave us shaking our heads in wonder on our way to find someone we can love like Jesus loves! When asked what she found strange about worship in our church, Marie said, "I thought worship was an internal matter. Why does everyone dress up? Why don't they just wear work clothes so that after they are amazed by God, they can go help people?" Sounds like worship to me!

Worship *must* be pursuit, for there is no way to fully catch God. I love the way Søren Kierkegaard puts it:

You have loved us first, O God, alas! We speak of it in terms of history as if You have only loved us first but a single time, rather than that without ceasing. You have loved us first many times and every day and our whole life through. When we wake up in the morning and turn our soul to you—You are the first—You have loved us first; if I

rise at dawn and at the same second turn my soul
toward You in prayer, You are there ahead of me.
You have loved me first. When I withdraw from
the distractions of the day and turn my soul to
You, You are the first and thus forever. And yet we
always speak ungratefully as if You have loved us
first only once.[24]

That is God-centered, God-pursuing worship!

Churches today that are most like the New Testament
church are the persecuted churches. They often find our
worship in the West to be strange. I have found that their
worship rarely focuses on feelings at all, but on declaring that
He is worthy to die for. This song from the Chinese underground church is typical:

I am willing to take up the cross and go forward
To follow the apostles down the road of sacrifice
That tens of thousands of precious souls can be saved
I am willing to leave all and be a martyr for the
    Lord

I love what we call "worship music." I listen to it all the
time. We sing it in our church. But I think the reason I

love it is that it moves *me*. And there's nothing wrong with that. But if authentic worship is knowing God for God's own sake, then perhaps we should join the persecuted church in worship that moves *Him*. That kind of worship would bring us into the middle of the purpose driven, purpose pursuing life.

FELLOWSHIP

When I asked Bob what he thought of when he heard the word *fellowship*, he said, "Frodo and the ring!" When I pressed him for a little more spiritual insight, he said, "Well, I never thought of fellowship related to church. Actually I never thought about church much at all. To me fellowship just means a place where no matter what I've done, I won't be ostracized."

Kind of tragic that Bob never saw the reality of that in a church, don't you think?

When I asked Marie the same question, she said, "Fellowship is the intimate space I have with God that I can share with another human being."

Great theologians could not have said better what fellowship should be.

Unfortunately, for many Christians fellowship has simply become another item on the to-do list. *Got to go to small group today so I can be accountable and get my needs met. Better go to Wednesday night service so I can get deeper teaching.* These things are important, but they are dead ends. If that's the way we view fellowship, then it ends as soon as the meeting is over. It's an arrival to a short-term parking place, and then we drive away to real life.

That's not fellowship!

Fellowship with God is to be known by Him as we are, to *know* that we are known by Him like this, and to know Him as *He* is. This *has* to be a journey. And the journey must then take us into the same kind of koinonia, life-sharing journey with each other. This kind of fellowship pursues each other into vulnerability, joy, anger, sadness, and love. It does not give up, move to another church because feelings were hurt, or settle for the surface.

One of the things I love most about the church where I am pastor is that we have been journeying for several years now into racial diversity. This is not an easy journey. We don't call it multicultural ministry but *cross*-cultural ministry. This is because we believe that God calls us to *cross over* into the lives and culture of others—to know who they *really* are. *It's exactly what Jesus did to save us!* Real fellowship is always cross-cultural. It models the Incarnation, as we take on the lives of those we love as our own. Would Bob and Marie find real fellowship with you? With your church? A place where they would never be ostracized, but would find that "intimate space with God to share with another human being"? If not, why don't you begin to change it? Start with one person. Or a few. Decide to know them and be known. Refuse to live without the community of real fellowship.

DISCIPLESHIP

Tozer writes about the training of the first disciples:

> The disciples were called, commissioned and taught in the best Bible school in the world, for there isn't a seminary on earth that can equal the seminary in which Jesus was the entire faculty! They didn't get a degree which they could frame and put on the wall, but they had a degree inside of them, and they loved Christ, our Lord. They loved Him living, they loved Him dead, and they loved Him living again.[25]

We tend to think of discipleship as a course or a curriculum, but for the first followers of Christ, *Jesus* was the curriculum! He was their story, their experience, their knowledge, and their journey. He was not their class. I'm not saying that we don't need teachers or that classes in themselves are bad, but the word *disciple* means one who follows a teacher. And ultimately, *Jesus* is to be that teacher.

I was amazed at Bob and Marie's response when I asked them about discipleship. I really wanted to see what Jesus alone was teaching them, since they hadn't yet had any real discipleship training. I asked Marie what she was learning about her new faith. She said, "I am learning so much. I am learning that Jesus is my teacher and my reward if I respond to Him, if I rely on Him 100 percent, if I believe. I am amazed by His interest in the details of my life. I am amazed to learn that He loves me that much. I cannot comprehend it."

Bob said, "I'm still in shock. A year ago my existence was the result of a pile of goo struck by lightning. Now I know I'm more than goo. I'm having to rewrite my whole view of the universe. Everything about everything! All of it must be seen from God's perspective. I studied anthropology. I could fit evolution and naturalism together until I broke out of the close-minded naturalistic box. Now the whole of the world is new!"

The whole of the world is new! What a statement. And what an opportunity.

Discipleship as pursuit is helping people, as Bob says, to see everything from God's perspective. When we meet as small groups, discipleship should be more of a lab environment where we can put to work what Jesus is teaching us. I asked Marie how she is learning about Jesus. "I learn by reading the Bible, freewriting my thoughts, and by silence knowing that Christ is in me. The more I do this, the more I learn to recognize His voice. I need to be able to recognize His voice from the others. There is another voice I hear which is sometimes beautiful, but it is an imitation. If I wait, it will crash like a wave and only fading foam will be left, and I will see that it is the voice of an enemy."

I didn't teach her any of this! Jesus really has been her teacher.

We must shift our view of discipleship from an expert imparting facts to a novice to helping people learn from Jesus Himself. *He* is the expert, and He can give insight to a baby believer that is more truthful than that coming from a great theologian. I am learning from Bob and Marie. And that's how it should be. Jesus personally taught His disciples, sent them out, and then they came back together. Luke 9:10 says, "When the apostles returned, they reported to Jesus what they had done. Then he took them with him and they withdrew by themselves."

Our discipleship groups and relationships should follow this pattern. Send people out to learn and serve. Bring them back together to share and point to Jesus as the Teacher. Going deeper in discipleship, then, will not mean just "learning more cool stuff we haven't heard yet." It will mean knowing Him and following Him on the real-life journey. As Eugene Peterson says, "Discipleship is anything that causes what is believed in the heart to have demonstrable consequences in our daily life."[26] This will never grow old or feel like a static system because we are not learning a system at all. We are knowing a Person!

MINISTRY

Bob and Marie were a little surprised to find out that it was the purpose of *their* lives to be ministers. Bob said, "I thought that was you!" But they were thrilled at the concept. Marie said, "I'm so encouraged that Jesus will use me—my words, my life—to pass on His love and His message by my caring for others." Have you heard a better definition of ministry than that?

They had no interest at all in ministry as a position. I am afraid that this is what we have often made it in the church—a job to be filled, a task to be done, something the preacher is nagging everyone about on Sunday. No wonder a younger generation doesn't like this concept. But that's not what ministry is or what *The Purpose Driven Life* teaches. It is a misperception we've created that we must destroy. Nothing will motivate postmoderns like ministry when it is taught and practiced as a journey of love, as opportunities waiting to surprise us around every corner—needs that can be met and lives that can be touched.

Bob and Marie have had a hard time engaging with our church. It's very different from their culture. We're exploring the idea of starting a postmodern, biblical church in their home. Though they struggle with many of the traditions of our church, they long to serve—to minister. They constantly ask how they can help, love, and touch lives. It is Jesus in them, drawing them to those He loves. Our thrilling opportunity in the church is to connect people with Jesus in practical ways that also connect them with the needs of others. We do not need to ask if people *have* their ministry, but rather, if ministry has *them* in such a way that every morning they embark on a new ministry adventure.

Ministry brings purposeful power to life in a way that the whole world can see. We must remember that most people live as if there is no resurrection realm to live in, no authentic power to receive. They exist this way because they have no spiritual eyes to see, and the church has not given them anything physical to see. Authentic ministry gives them the physical to see that can draw them to the spiritual they are blind to.

As I write this chapter, I am in Wales with my good friend Rhys Stenner, pastor of Holland Road Baptist Church in Brighton, England. We are having an incredible time. We are meeting with pastors and leaders for one-day leadership seminars in different parts of Wales. We have been working with them for a few years now to seek God for a fresh work of power in this land. Thrilling things are beginning to happen.

One hundred years ago, Wales experienced one of the greatest movements of God's Spirit in history. The entire nation was transformed by the Welsh Revival of 1904. Indeed, the whole world was impacted by it. The spiritual heritage of the nation remains today. Rhys told me of his recent experience attending the rugby game between Wales and New Zealand. One hundred thousand people filled the stadium, and the national fervor was at fever pitch. Before the game began, the Welsh crowd sang the unofficial national song at the top of their lungs. Rhys showed me a video of the game. Otherwise I might not have believed it. Children, women, and tough old Welshmen alike were bellowing with all their hearts—and they were singing a hymn! "Guide Me, O Thou Great Jehovah." It was an amazing thing to see. Can you imagine if one year at the Super Bowl the crowd broke into song and sang, "Bread of heaven, bread of heaven, feed me till I want no more! Feed me till I want no more"?

Sadly, though the spiritual heritage of this nation remains, the spiritual life has gone. That night, in my hotel room, I watched a special on the musical history of Wales. The narrator commented on how beloved this hymn is throughout the country, even today. But then he said, "No one in Wales appears to need the Jehovah they sing about. No one wants to feed on the bread of heaven anymore."

I wanted to cry. I understand what the narrator meant, but I just don't believe it's true. I believe that in Wales—and in the whole earth—people are longing for the bread of heaven. But they're not sure if it is real, because they haven't seen much of the Baker. And that is not the Baker's fault. He has one plan to enable the world to want His bread—the church must distribute it to hungry people. And we do that through ministry.

When people see the adventure of our ministries, the sheer joy we have at the opportunity to comfort a widow, mentor a child, repair a dilapidated school, visit prisoners, bring food to the hungry, care for a pregnant teenager, nurse a lonely AIDS victim, and be a friend to the friendless, they will not just sing about the bread of heaven with a faint memory of its aroma; they will consume it. And then they will sing a new song! That is the joy of ministry—not a task to be done, but a journey of love to embark on. That's what the purpose driven, purpose pursuing life looks like.

EVANGELISM

I don't believe there is any greater joy in my life than evangelism. Who doesn't love to tell good news? Why wouldn't people want to spend their days doing it? Maybe because we have made evangelism sound like bad news so many times and because we approach it as our "job" rather than our joy. I have done evangelism just about every way possible, but I have to confess that I don't find many evangelistic methods of yesterday to be effective today.

We have often turned evangelism into a course to learn. We finish the course and then we go "hunting" for lost people to use our newfound "skills" and "techniques" on. I have taken all the courses. I have learned much from them, but most of the time I wonder if we aren't missing the Jesus way. Jesus evangelized *as He went*. He shared with a man in a tree He met by the side of the road, with a woman getting Him some water, with some people He saw fishing, and with a tax collector at work. When the tax collector Matthew became His follower, He immediately sent him to get all his friends and have a dinner party at his house. Jesus shared while He ate with them. This all sounds very different to me than most of the ways we do evangelism.

Now, I don't want to discourage anyone who is effective in sharing Christ. That is my heart and my passion. It just seems to me that anything we do is better when modeled after Jesus' way. And Jesus shared through love and relationship. I do most of my evangelism training in restaurants. I often take people with me to my favorite haunt and show them how easy and truly wonderful it is to make new friends and care for every part of their lives. I have made so many friends like Marie through simply caring for people who are serving me.

I never share the gospel with strangers, though I often share with those I have just met. I believe that God loves the people I will meet today more than I do and He will give supernatural connections that will give us an immediate bond of friendship. Then I am not sharing with a stranger, but a friend, and no one is more ready to listen than a friend. I have so many long-term relationships with good friends who don't know Christ that I never lack for people to share the Good News with. And I never went and "hunted" for any of these friends. I found them in the natural course of my life. I asked Marie how someone could have told her the Good News in a way she would have received.

"I needed to see that the messenger really cared about me," she said. "I didn't want him to be condescending. I wanted him to listen a lot, to talk to me about Jesus, but *live* it more. I needed to see the evidence of the living Christ in Him. And I wanted someone to really care for my soul. You see, Jesus is a soul matter, not to be settled over one talk."

What if every follower of Christ viewed evangelism as the normal process of making friends, loving people like Jesus did, and sharing good news only with people who actually want to hear it? I believe we would see the Spirit of God sweep through our schools, marketplaces, and neighborhoods. Evangelism would become a wonderful part of the journey, not an assignment to dread. I love going to lunch with my friend Ed. He's eighty-one years old, and I have learned so much from him about times I was not alive to see. He still would have been my friend had he never met Jesus. But praying with him recently to receive Christ after lunch one day filled me with so much joy. Do you know what it's like to tell a son that his father just met Jesus after the son has prayed for his dad all his life? You never get over that.

If you want to really see evangelism come alive for you so that you wonder how you ever had joy without it, go to the mission field for a few weeks. Watch the power of God move in places where people are desperate for Him. Watch Him use you. Watch Him fill you with love for a people you have never met or even known anything about. You will be living out the pursuing love of Jesus then. And when you get back, people will wonder why you went. When you spill over with excitement about what you experienced (and you will), people will want to know more. They will know this is real to you if it took you to the other side of the world. They will then be ready to hear about it on this side of the world. Bob knows all about my mission travel. He said to me, "You took the weakness out of Christianity, John. I always viewed it as weak. But you run around the Middle East! Once the weakness was taken out, it was easy for me to look in."

Honestly, this intentional, daily journey of evangelism is so much fun that I can't believe most believers miss it. It will lead you into relationships and experiences that will become the highlights of your life. Like the day I baptized Bob and Marie—in my unheated outdoor swimming pool, in February! You see, Marie had read the story of Jesus' baptism and informed me that He was not baptized in an indoor pool and she wanted to really follow Him. That was an experience! Or the first time Bob and Marie took the Lord's Supper.

Bob and Marie have become such good friends that they have spent the last Christmas and Good Friday with our family. On Good Friday, we had a nontraditional service in our home in which we moved from room to room telling the story of the last days of Jesus. We began in our dining room with the Lord's Supper. Marie was sitting next to me. As I broke the bread and gave it to her, it hit me. "Marie, do you remember what you were doing when we first met?"

Wide-eyed, she realized what I was talking about. "I was serving *you* bread," she said.

This is the life, the sheer joy we get when we journey with Jesus into the lives of people who need to know Him. This is the wonderful way evangelism empowers us with purpose and makes our lives good news to all who see us coming.

NOT YET

The resurrection realm is calling you—to pursue your purpose by taking hold of all that for which Christ took hold of you. You've not arrived. And that's all right. You will one day. The end of the movie *Gladiator* is one of the most powerful and emotional conclusions in cinematic history. The hero, Maximus, while mortally wounded, kills the evil, usurping emperor, setting all of Rome free from his murderous grip. He then falls dying. As he slips away, he sees his murdered wife and son waiting for him in the afterlife. His friend and a former slave says, "Now we are free. I will see you again. But not yet. Not yet."

The pursuit will end one day. You will catch all of God—all His power, the fullness of all His purpose. You will see Him face to face, like He *is*. But *not yet*. And the "not yet" is good—it is the journey into empowered purpose.

CHAPTER SEVEN

LIVING BETWEEN THE CHAPTERS

*Brothers, I do not consider myself yet to have
taken hold of it. But one thing I do...*

PHILIPPIANS 3:13

*The ability to concentrate—to persevere on
a course without distraction or diversion—
is a power that has enabled men of moderate
capability to reach heights of attainment
that have eluded the genius.*

R. ALEC MACKENZIE

I n between the last chapter and this one, my whole
life changed.

After I finished writing the last chapter, I had a
decision to make. Before I started this one, I made that
decision and the entire direction of my ministry changed.
For the first time in twenty-five years, I am not the pastor

of a church. I am the vice president for evangelization of
the North American Mission Board. I am thrilled about
the new challenge to which God has called me, but that's
not what I want to write about. What happened "between
the chapters" is what's really important.

It seems to me that most of us will face a handful of
transitions in our life that will largely determine how God
uses us, what the course of our life will be, and whether
we live that life in the resurrection realm of God's power.
Think of the phenomenal importance of key transitional
decisions in the lives of biblical characters.

Abraham is enjoying a decent life in Haran, getting
ready for retirement. Would he really obey God and leave
his home, not even knowing where he was going? And
what would be the cost to the world if he had not?

Noah is minding his own business and living a good
life. Would he really listen to this crazy plan of God's
and embarrass himself in front of everyone by building
a big boat? And what would be the cost to the world if
he had not?

A group of amazed followers of the risen Christ stood
on a mountain and watched Him ascend. He had just
commissioned them to go to the world with His love. All
their own plans were now obsolete! Would they really

leave everything behind and risk their lives to follow the One they could no longer see? Would they become His missionaries? And what would be the cost to the world if they had not?

God, wrapped up in weeping, bleeding, terrified human flesh, knelt alone in a dark garden. Would He really follow through with this and bear our sins on the cross? And what would be the cost to the world—to you, to me—if He had not?

Many others faced similar transitions and made the wrong choice—men like Cain, Saul, Judas, and the rich young ruler. These choices are real—and the consequences are real too. You are living in a particular chapter of life right now. The time will come when the opportunity will present itself to close the last page of that chapter and open up the first page of the next one. How do you know if the time is right? How do you look ahead and distinguish between stepping into a dark chapter of bad choices and a new chapter of God's adventure for you, full of resurrection power? What you do in those moments and days of living between the chapters, of facing life's critical transitions, will follow you for good or bad for the rest of your days.

My son and I enjoy going to scary movies. Occasionally, one that's fit to see comes out, and Trey and

I go. We went recently, and the theater was nearly full. The movie was new and interest was high. I *think* the movie was really bad, though I am not certain because I have no idea what it was about. I watched the entire movie and cannot think of one thing I understood. And it didn't help that it was an un-scary scary movie. I did laugh a few times, but that was also bad since it wasn't supposed to be funny!

The movie was so convoluted that I thought it was going to be one of those films with a surprise ending that brought it all together and suddenly made sense of it all. Instead, the main characters drove into a dark tunnel and the credits rolled. At that moment I knew I wasn't the only one thinking how bad this movie was. The audience began to shout things at the screen. "That was terrible!" "I just threw away my money!" "I just wasted two hours!" Several began to curse. This continued until the whole theater was filled with shouting, angry people. I'd never seen anything like it. My son and I slipped out to escape what appeared to be a riot in the making.

As we left I thought, *Wouldn't it be terrible to be the director or an actor in that movie and hear* that? But what if life were a movie? It's certainly an adventure fit for the big screen. What if all of heaven were watching it—your life on film? And if at the end they shouted, "That was terrible! What a waste!"? If that were to happen, it would probably be because you made terrible choices at key transitions. But that is not God's script for you. He is with you between the chapters—helping you see where you have been and where you are going and guiding you into wise transitions in the key moments of life. So let's talk about that. How do we keep our story consistent with God's script so that the next chapters, all the way to the final chapter, release His power in our story?

I love the quotes of Winston Churchill. He was gifted in the art of quick wit. One evening as he was leaving a bar he encountered his nemesis in Parliament, Bessie Braddock. "Winston," she said icily, "you're drunk!" Churchill straightened up and said, "Madam, you're ugly. But tomorrow I shall be sober!" There are some things that you cannot change! But the next chapter of your life is not one of them. You can turn the page and walk into power.

THE TRANSITION TEST

The next time you find yourself between the chapters, *ask yourself three questions before you make a move.* Answer these questions well and I'm convinced you'll make wise decisions that will ensure your next chapter will be lived in the same power Jesus had as He stepped out of the tomb.

WHAT AM I BUILDING?

"Brothers, I do not consider myself…"

Within these words is more power than you could use in a hundred lifetimes. And yet most of that power goes completely unused. We are so programmed to "consider ourselves" first in every major decision. The *Word Study New Testament* says that the Greek word *consider* means "to put together with one's mind." What if when we faced significant transitions, we broke the mold and refused to put it all together with our own mind, to figure out what makes the best sense to us and do it? What if instead we looked far beyond ourselves and asked God what He wants to do with this decision in a thousand years?

I love castles. Their stories and mysteries fascinate me. Recently I took two trips within a few weeks and was able to see a castle on both trips. The first was a mission trip to Wales. It was my second time in Wales, and I could not wait to visit Cardiff Castle again. It is a magnificent castle, right out of a fairy tale, and I needed some time alone there. I had a free afternoon so I caught a bus to Cardiff.

It was very cold and not many others were dumb enough to sit in a castle tower that day, which was fine with me. I had come there to be alone with God. I was facing a huge decision: Should I take this new position and leave the pastorate, my church family, and all my comfort zones?

I looked at the walls—walls whose foundations were built in Roman times. Walls that had stood for generations. I thought about the fact that the first builders of this castle never saw it completed. In fact, they probably couldn't even have dreamed of its final form. It was bigger than them. They had built for a day they would never see. God began to speak to my heart about the condition of the culture of North America and the desperate need for His people to follow Him in fresh ways to bring His message to those who do not know Him. Right then I couldn't see God's final design to turn North America back to Him. Still can't. But I began to hear His call to be His bricklayer, to join my heart and hands with anyone else who felt the same call—to build God's castle.

A few weeks later, I was on a beautiful beach with my family on vacation. A sudden storm came up, and I hurried down the beach toward shelter. Suddenly I stopped in my tracks. There before me was another castle. As the wind-driven rain pelted my back, I stood and stared. I'm sure people around thought I was nuts, standing in the rain and staring—at a sand castle! But I heard God's whisper. "Watch this," He said. "Watch how quickly the rain and rising waves wash all this away. Your plans, no matter how impressive they are, are sand castles. Come with Me, come My way. Build what will stand."

And my call was confirmed. I could stay at my wonderful church. I could avoid all the uncertainty, the change, the parting from friends. But I would hurt those I loved. I would hurt my church by staying. Anything we build *here* when God has called us to go *there* is a sand castle. I am excited about the future of the church that I have called home. I am excited about the new direction—the next chapter—of my life. But these decisions are so hard, aren't they? It is so difficult to "not consider myself" and to take God's castle-tower view. But the keys to power are found there.

At Cardiff Castle, I purchased several sets of replica castle keys. In just a few weeks, I will be going on an annual campout with my son, my dad, my brother and brother-in-law, and their boys. It's a highlight of our year. Around the fire one night, I will give each of the boys a set of those castle keys. And we will talk about the keys to making wise decisions in life. God's castle keys are in your hands too. He wants you to know His will and His mighty power. As you face the big transitions of life, ask the big question, the hard question, and answer it with all the honesty in your heart: *Which decision will allow you to build a lasting castle, not a sand castle?* Which decision will stand for a thousand years? Which decision is bigger than you?

Make *that* choice. Power is there! God is there.

WHAT AM I REALLY REACHING FOR?

"Brothers, I do not consider myself *yet to have taken hold of it...*"

As you stand between the chapters, about to write the next one in your life, what are you *really* reaching for? This is a critical question. You must clearly and honestly know your heart to make wise transitional decisions. Why are you considering this option? Are you running from something? Are you running after something? If so, what?

Remember what Paul is talking about when he says he has *yet to have taken hold of it.* He's talking about authentic power! He is ready to move forward to a different place for the right reason. To walk with Jesus in the same strength He had as He came out of the tomb. Can you make this decision and move into a new chapter of life, walking with Him *into* resurrection power? Will this decision lead you to His *deeper* power? Will you have to depend on Him more or less? *Can you do this without Him?* These are the kinds of key questions you must answer to be sure you are reaching for the right things in your decision making. Otherwise you can find yourself just reaching for more stuff or more ego strokes or more of what someone else has that you don't.

And that's a dangerous, dead-end street.

Don't misunderstand me. Financial and material issues are not unimportant. God expects us to work and is not unconcerned about our daily needs. He is the One who meets them! And He is not a dull, somber God whose will is for all our decisions to lead to a harder life. In fact, the Bible tells us that God is the one who "richly provides us with everything for our enjoyment" (1 Timothy 6:17).

The problem comes when these things become your goals, when your decisions are made based first and foremost on what you can get out of it. Joy comes as a wonderful by-product of following Jesus in your decisions. If your first thoughts or your most important thoughts about your transitional decisions involve how much money you will make or what you will get out of it, you may be in danger of turning the page and moving into the wrong chapter.

Do you want a great picture of a man who made a huge

decision the right way, reaching for the right thing? Jim Elliot, the missionary martyr who helped launch the modern missions movement, was making his decision to go witness to the dangerous Auca Indians—a decision that cost him his life but has resulted in the saved lives and the eternities of thousands being changed forever. He wrote this in his journal during that transitional time:

> [He makes] His ministers a flame of fire. Am I ignitable? God deliver me from the dread asbestos of "other things." Saturate me with the oil of the Spirit that I may be aflame. But flame is transient, often short-lived. Canst thou bear this, my soul—short life? In me there dwells the Spirit of the Great Short-Lived, whose zeal for God's house consumed Him. Make me Thy fuel, Flame of God.[27]

That puts it all together for me. Am I willing to make the big decisions of life with the pure motive of being His fuel? Don't let *other things* become asbestos in your life. Don't let anything insulate you from the power of God. You have one life. It may be short or shorter, but in the scheme of things it is not long. Not long at all. Make every decision count!

IS THIS WORTH JESUS' FOCUS?

"But one thing I do…"

It's so important for you to understand this simple statement from God's Word. Paul simply says, "But one thing…" *One thing.* Clear focus was his goal, and it must be ours. But whose focus are we pursuing? If we pursue our own, we may be driven but not by resurrection power. It is Jesus' focus we are after. If we look only through His eyes at the road ahead, we will always know the right direction to take. *One thing.*

You might be surprised to know that in this passage, the word *one* does not mean "one." Huh? Stick with me. It doesn't refer to the "number" one. The *Word Study New Testament* points out that when used in this form, it means "one in essence," not the number one. Finding your "one thing" doesn't just mean choosing a particular focus and concentrating all your energies on it. It means lining up your focus with the essence of who you are meant to be. And the Bible leaves no doubt about who you are to be.

Just before Jesus was arrested, He prayed for you. Yes, for *you*. In John 17, Jesus specifically prays for all those through the years who would believe in Him. He prays to His Father more than once that we will *be one*, as He and

His Father are one (vv. 21–22). And then He immediately tells us what that means: "I in them and you in me" (v. 23). The Father lives out His focus through the Son, and the Son intends to live out His focus through us. And when we stay in this amazing relationship, the power of God protects us from turning the page on the wrong chapter. Listen to another of Jesus' prayers for you: "Holy Father, protect them by the *power* of your name—the name you gave me—so that they may be *one* as we are one" (v. 11).

So as you face the major transition decisions, ask the right questions. Would Jesus make this course of action His focus? Can you do this *with* Jesus? He in you and you in Him? Is this choice *worth Jesus' focus?*

As you begin to make decisions this way, power will follow you. When you are one with Him, you will grow in unity with His family and your power will multiply. The first believers quickly learned this secret. When they became "*one* in heart and mind," "great power" was all over them, all around them (Acts 4:32–33). And they immediately began to use that power to share the resurrection power of Christ with others. "With great power the apostles continued to testify to the resurrection of the Lord Jesus, and much grace was upon them all" (v. 33).

If you ever find yourself really stuck in a key decision

and the way forward to Jesus' focus is just not clear, ask yourself which course of action will allow you the greatest opportunity to love others and share Christ's love with them. That will almost always be the right choice. How can I be so sure? Because Jesus leaves the ninety-nine sheep to find the one. If He died for the lost and He lives in you, don't you think His road forward for you will always lead to someone who needs His love? And as you take this road, such joy, power, and glory will fill you that it almost seems selfish. I love what Michael Simpson says in *Permission Evangelism*: "The act of loving others awakens God's Spirit in us and our purpose is realized. The gaps are filled; God smiles and we are enveloped in His glory."[28]

Yes! That's the path to take.

Here's a wonderful truth. God is not hiding His will from you. In fact, the opposite is true. He is after you, to center your life on His focus. You see it all through His life. He was after the heart of a rich young ruler. He told him that he lacked "one thing" (Luke 18:22). He told His dear friend Martha, who was distracted by so many things, that only "one thing" was needed (10:42). Even if you are too blind to see the road forward, to see the page of the next chapter, Jesus still seeks you, to give you the "one thing" focus. He stopped at the side of a poor blind beggar one day and gave him sight. And surrounded by the enemies of Christ who cursed him and threw him out of their presence, the man rose up in courage and said, "*One thing* I do know. I was blind but now I see!" (John 9:25). He got more than his sight. He got his focus—on Jesus. And you can too.

THE CHAPTER OF RESURRECTION POWER

That's the chapter you're looking to write. Whatever your last chapter has been like, God wants your next one to be lived in the resurrection realm. He wants to show you power you've never seen. And He wants to show the world His power through you. Don't be surprised when that power comes painfully. Remember chapter 3? We die with Him before we rise in power with Him.

My good friend Woody Johnson and I were talking about this one day. Woody said, "God told me I had to be a dead man. I said, 'Great!' But I had no idea how painful it is to die." Woody's right. And we must die to many lesser things to find His one thing. That can be painful, but it is also powerful. Powerful enough to change the course of history.

I am convinced that God is ready for a fresh move of His power in our day. It has been a long time. Too long. I see the hunger growing. Even desperation. People are starting to really believe that without a surprising God-intervention in our culture, we are ruined. We are done. Finished. The good news is that God has done it before. And when God intervenes, He does it through ordinary people—who turn the right way at the crossroads of life and become vessels of His power.

Few people have been less likely to be used by God to change history than William Wilberforce. He was born sickly and almost blind in 1759. His father died when he was nine, and his mother, who was unable to care for him, gave him to relatives. He was brilliant, however—a gifted orator, and elected to the British Parliament as a young man. In spite of this incredible opportunity, he began to throw his life away in gambling and drinking. But God was seeking him, drawing him.

In a meeting with the converted slave trader and writer of "Amazing Grace," John Newton, Wilberforce met Christ and was transformed. And the Spirit of Christ in him led him to turn the page into a new chapter—one that would last the rest of his life and would change the world. Wilberforce set out to abolish slavery in England. It seemed an impossible task. His friends abandoned him. He was beaten on the streets. Assassins sought to kill him. But he had found his focus—Jesus' focus—and he would not turn the pages to an easier chapter.

In 1788 he made his first motion in Parliament to abolish slavery. He lost then and kept losing year after year. After five years of defeats, he received a letter from one of the greatest men of his day. John Wesley, the great revival leader, was eighty-eight and near death. But he had something to say. In an amazing letter written to Wilberforce one week before he died, Wesley said:

> Unless God has raised you up for this very thing, you will be worn out by the opposition of men and devils, but if God be for you who can be against you? Are all of them together stronger than God? Oh be not weary of well-doing. Go on in the name of God, and in the *power* [emphasis mine] of His might, till even American slavery (the vilest that ever saw the sun) shall vanish away before it....
>
> That He that has guided you from your youth up may continue to strengthen in this and all things, is the prayer of, dear sir,
>
> Your affectionate servant, John Wesley[29]

And Wilberforce didn't quit. Not for forty more years. The night he died, in 1833, the House of Commons passed the Emancipation Clause that set all slaves free. He had won. Jesus had won through him. He opened a new chapter—not just for himself, but for generations to come.

And now, as I turn the pages of one chapter of my life, I see a once all-Anglo church that now has two hundred African American members and more coming every month. And I go to a new work where part of my responsibility will be cross-cultural evangelism—to join hands with those whose ancestors were enslaved, to break the chains of darkness for those of every color. Thank you, William! Two hundred years after your death, your courage impacts my life every day.

And what might happen if thousands or millions of believers found their essence, their "one thing" focus, and refused ever to turn in another direction? The world would change! In as many ways as there are believers who would follow Jesus to where the change is needed. That is the hope of the world. And the hope is real indeed.

The transitions of life are coming. The choices that will make all the difference. And Jesus will be there to meet you for every one of them. He will stand with you between the chapters until it's time to turn the page. Let's learn together how to move forward with Jesus, stepping out of the tomb and into the story that He is writing with the pen of your life.

CHAPTER EIGHT

BREAKING THE POWER OF THE PAST

Forgetting what is behind...

PHILIPPIANS 3:13

If your horse is dead, for goodness' sake, dismount!

EDDY KETCHURSID

Many of us are trying to ride dead horses to powerful places. The horse was so powerful in the past. We love the horse so much. For some, it's the only horse we've ever known. We've never ridden any other horse.

For whatever reason, we just can't bring ourselves to get off that thing. So we sit on its dead back, prodding it and stroking it. Sometimes we prop it up so it looks alive. We climb back on it and tell ourselves it's only been sleeping. Any minute now it will spring into action. And we'll stay right there on its rotting back—proudly.

As people pass by, they occasionally try to point out that our horse is dead. We usually get angry and defensive and criticize their "new" horse. We aren't comfortable being the only one on a dead horse, and so we offer conferences on "Riding Boldly into the Future!" All the dead-horse owners arrive, dragging their horse carcasses behind them. They climb on their dead bodies and shout loudly about the coming stampede of their horses—any minute now they will arise and charge. We'd better be ready.

Occasionally, a young man on a young colt accidentally wanders in. Because he is the only one actually moving forward on a living creature, he is quite conspicuous at the conference. He doesn't stay long though. He clearly doesn't fit in. A few encourage him to stay. "This conference needs some young riders," they say. But when the young rider points out that there is a whole ranch of living horses just down the street, and that he would show anyone who wanted one where they were and how to ride them, the response is lukewarm at best. So he begins to ride away. He has places to go and can't afford to waste time. And anyway—that smell!

"The conference has gone well," all the dead horse owners say to each other, as they shoo away flies. And everyone says that this year's horse wax is the best yet. It puts such an attractive sheen on their hides. And the best part, they say as they drag their horses out the door, is that it comes in a lovely, "back to the old barnyard" aroma.

I wish I didn't have to tell this story. Because, as you can probably tell, it is a parable of the church today. And I love the church. I have given my life to her. She is the bride of Christ, meant to be vibrant and alive. And too much is at stake for us to act like the church is just fine. We are in desperate trouble. We oppose secular culture but find it much harder to love, engage, and reach those living in it. We are internally focused. We are rotting, stinking, and we hardly notice or care. The lyrics from an old Lynyrd Skynyrd song describe it so well: "Ooh ooh, that smell! Can't you smell that smell? Ooh ohh, that smell. The smell of death's around you." We treat our methodologies as sacred, as if we had written them into the Bible itself. We are becoming more and more like the Pharisees, and that is inexcusable. *Because we are meant for power!*

As I speak at churches around the country, I am stunned at the number that are willing to continue with business as usual even though it is clear that they are dying. Pastors are discouraged and their people are comfortable as long as they can ride their own familiar dead horse all the way to their graves.

If reading this is uncomfortable for you, know that my goal is not to make anyone mad. But I won't pander to dead-horse churches or dead-horse Christians. And you shouldn't either. Aren't you hungering for authentic power? Isn't that why you're reading?

People and churches that live in the past will never find it, which is exactly what the religious authorities tried to get the early church to do. They pursued early Christians and killed them because they wouldn't stay on the dead horses of legalism or idolatry. But the early church knew that the power of the resurrection was worth *more* than what the world could do to them. And because of their passion for authentic power, they were willing to follow Jesus anywhere and in new ways. They came out of the tomb with Him and *left the dead past in there!*

We need to learn how to do this. We need to be *willing* to do this. Because we don't have much time to decide to get off the dead horse and ride with Christ.

Before we talk about how to leave our dead past behind, let me point out that there is another reason some stay on a different breed of dead horses. Many would love to dismount, but they don't know they can. They have ridden dead horses of the past for so long—guilt, shame, bitterness, and sometimes even success-generated pride—that they believe it's the only horse they are ever meant to ride. But both groups have a wonderful opportunity before them—to break the power of the past and move into a life of real power!

LEAVE YOUR GRAVE CLOTHES

I know what we all mean when we talk about the "empty tomb." But the Bible never says the tomb is *empty*. In fact, it specifically says that after Jesus rose, the tomb was *not* empty. When Peter arrived at the tomb, "he saw the strips of linen lying there, as well as the burial cloth that had been around Jesus' head" (John 20:6–7). And here's a good trivia question: What was in the "empty" tomb that weighed seventy-five pounds? "Nicodemus brought a mixture of myrrh and aloes, about seventy-five pounds" (19:39).

So when Jesus rose, He left behind grave clothes and perfume. So what?

Let's remember what we're after—authentic power. We want to live in the same power Jesus had as He walked out of the tomb. The question is, what do *we* leave in the tomb to step out of it in power? It's important because our authentic-power passage says to forget "that which is behind."

The word translated *behind* is an interesting one. Its most common meaning in the Gospels is "to follow." Seven times Jesus commands people to follow Him using this word. In Matthew 4:19, He says, "Come, *follow* me, and I will make you fishers of men." In Luke 9:23, He says, "If anyone would come after me, he must deny himself and take up his cross daily and *follow* me." So Jesus calls us to follow Him, to be like Him in His resurrection, which means we must leave behind what He leaves behind.

When Jesus went into the tomb, He was wearing the grave clothes of a dead man. In his death, He carried all the guilt, shame, and sin of the world into that tomb. But when He came out, He left it all behind. Jesus calls you to follow Him and to leave all your sin and foolish pride where it belongs—as grave clothes inside the tomb, where Jesus has broken their power. You don't have to ride that dead, powerless horse any longer.

Jesus' body was also covered with perfume to hide the stench of death. But when He came out of the tomb, he no longer needed anything to cover the smell of death. He walked out in new, vibrant life and left the perfumes useless in the tomb. Jesus calls you to follow—to leave behind all the artificial ways you have perfumed your dead horse and to ride into new life and real power.

It sounds scary, doesn't it? But you can do it. Churches can do it. There's room in the tomb for all of your past! But let's not be too symbolic. Let's get practical. How do you break the power of the past—right now?

FORGETFUL FAITH

In chapter 4, we saw that resurrection power comes to us like salvation does—by faith. We already possess it because we already possess the Spirit of power. But we have to walk in it by faith. It is the only way. Faith is the language of authentic power. Seeking power any other way just won't translate into the power Jesus brought out of the tomb with Him.

Let's see how to actually use our faith. The necessity of faith is never seen more clearly than in what it takes to break the power of the past. *"Forgetting* that which is behind..." What does this mean? Does God want us to have spiritual Alzheimer's? Of course not. *Forgetting* does not mean to have no memory of something. In fact, it requires you to know what is in your past. It means to consciously and intensely neglect something. It means to look squarely at your past and decide to view it as Christ does—no matter how *you* feel about it. It is the picture of faith.

Elisabeth Elliot gives the best definition I have seen of the kind of faith that breaks the power of the past: "Real faith trusts absolutely. Real faith is a *willed choice*, made in the very teeth of adversity."[30] A willed choice. Now that's exciting! Because if the power of God is already in me, then I have the strength to choose what to do with the past. And if it is my choice, then nothing in the past can control or enslave me. I am free!

I don't think I can stress enough how important this next step is for you—and for the kingdom of God. The church is God's only plan—if it turns away from the resurrection power in which it was meant to live, there is no Plan B! And the church is *you* and those you share fellowship with.

All that God wants to do in and through you and your church is at stake. God has chosen to *need* you. And Jesus has spoken clearly: "No one who puts his hand to the plow and looks back is fit for service in the kingdom of God" (Luke 9:62). *Back* is the same word in the Greek as *behind*. We have to clearly see what part of the past has been holding us back from the power of His kingdom and then *forget*, intentionally and intensely neglect, those things "which are behind."

We come to a decisive moment: Resurrection power is our choice. The kingdom of God awaits. The King leads the way. We are ready for our willed choice, by faith to break free from the past. Let's do it!

Stop where you are. Get alone. Be honest. First, ask God if you have grave clothes that need to be left in the tomb. Have you let the enemy constantly remind you of your past sin, your guilt, your shame? Are you bitter and angry toward those you believe have wronged you, unwilling to really forgive even though you want Christ to forgive *you*? Do you live with constant insecurity and fear because of what others have done to you? Have you believed the lies others have told you—that you are worthless, unloved, unworthy? Will you continue to live in this past and call Jesus a liar when He says that you are a friend of God, even a *child* of God?

Or maybe your grave clothes are a little different. Maybe you enjoy the perfume that is smeared on them. Maybe you have not been willing to even notice that they weigh seventy-five pounds and are dragging like an anchor, keeping you from kingdom power. Do you refuse to move forward into what God is doing today because you want

Him to do it the way He did it yesterday—your way? Are you living a pride-driven life because you will not allow God to be God, and create His own future? Are you stuck in a past that you have sealed in your mind as "the good days," so that you are in danger of missing God's days that are ahead for you?

THE POWER PROMISE PRAYER

If you're willing to be honest and you see yourself still wearing grave clothes, it's time to take them off by faith and walk out of the tomb in Jesus' power! Are you ready? Pray this prayer or something like it:

Jesus, I'm tired of missing Your resurrection power because I'm living in the past. I am ready to take off these grave clothes and follow You into the real life you have for me. By faith I do it right now! I reject all the enemy's lies about my past. I am forgiven and free just as You have told me. I reject the lies that I have come to believe because of what others have done to me. I reject bitterness and anger and foolish pride and everything else that keeps me stuck in the past. I ask you to cleanse me and break the power of the past in Jesus' name. By faith, I will forget what is behind.

Lord, I desire to leave my comfort zones, to no longer insist that You do things my way or the way You have done them in the past. Do whatever You want, in whatever way You want, and do it in me! And do it in my church, Lord. Change everything and anything, Lord. I want to know the power of Your resurrection. I want it more than anything. Your Word is Truth. It is my constant. And in it is the promise that Your Spirit is on the move, always working in new ways and in mighty power. I want in on it, O God! Right now. For Your honor. For Your glory. For the sake of Your bride. For the sake of Your kingdom. My hand is on the plow. My heart is set. My eyes are on You. I'm not looking back! In Jesus' name, amen.

Now share this with your friends. With your pastor. With your church. Start a movement. Bury the dead horses. And let's leave the tomb for resurrection power. Just imagine what can be—what will be—if we do!

POWER IS YOUR DESTINY

It really is, you know. Jesus has promised it to you. There is no reason to miss it, and in fact, you can't. Power is your destiny. The only question is whether power will be *in* you or *over* you.

Jude 1:7 says, "Sodom and Gomorrah and the surrounding towns *gave themselves up*." Two entire cities chose to give themselves to what should have been far behind them. And though they could have had power *in* them, they experienced tragic, destructive power *over* them. If you choose to keep your weighed-down, perfumed grave clothes on, your destruction may not be as immediate or as visual as Sodom and Gomorrah's, but the decay and rot have set in. You may not even see it. The most tragic thing a believer can experience is to walk out of God's power and begin to self-destruct, blind to what so many around them can clearly see.

I saw it happen in the life of one of the most gifted and caring people I have ever known. I genuinely loved him and still do. I pray for him often. He bears many wounds from his past, and though many people have prayed and pleaded with him, even his good friends, he will not leave the old wounds in the tomb. As a result, he is eaten alive with bitterness. He plots against wonderful people that he imagines are his enemies. He goes from failure to failure and refuses to accept responsibility. He slanders and attacks and gossips. But in the next breath, he will care for those who others might ignore.

He seems entirely blind to the destructive power that can engulf him. And yet He is my brother—and so full of the potential for resurrection power God has placed in him. I pray regularly for him and others who seem to be always *remembering* the things which are behind. And I ask God to remind me that I could be one of them. And be blind to my own grave clothes. I know this power is my destiny—either in me or over me. And I am after the resurrection power that is in me.

HAVE A *SIP* OF POWER

This section of the book is one of my favorite things to write about, talk about, and think about. In fact, if this section excites you, you might want to check out my book *The Passion Promise*, which really expounds on the joy God has in giving us a life of passion. This is where pursuing resurrection power gets really fun. (It's not all fun, remember. Suffering and death come before resurrection.) But when we really begin to see the invisible power of the resurrection realm invade our lives in ways we can't miss—well, there's nothing like it! And the God of love and overflowing joy desires this for you.

What is a SIP of power? I believe Scripture teaches that if God poured out all His power and glory on us, we would simply collapse and die. It is too much for us in these limited, mortal bodies. One day we will be eternally equipped to take it all in, but for now God gives us small tastes of His power. We sometimes call these tastes *miracles,* but that terminology can imply that God almost never works that way. Scripture reveals that God's *normal* method of operation is to show His power to His people. It's just that we're rarely ready to see it. But when we are, when we have set our hearts on living in the resurrection realm, where power is the norm, we can expect to see God faithfully demonstrate His power. When He does this in memorable, faith-building ways, I call these SIPs:

Sacred
Intimate
Places

These are holy moments when God is more real than the air we breathe. He *is* the air we breathe. That moment, that physical or spiritual place, becomes sacred and intimate because God brought you there to love you, to build your faith, to shower you, His child, with Himself. Sacred, intimate places of power. Faith-boosters that guard you from ever turning from the resurrection realm to lesser plains. Why would anyone want to, when they can wake up every day and know that God will be at work in all they do and that the next SIP of power is just around the corner?

SIPs often come when we make decisions to follow Jesus by faith into new territories, forgetting the past. One of my favorite personal SIPs happened about six years ago. I had been deeply involved in mission work in Belarus for many years. I had seen so many wonderful things and had made lifetime friends, even learning a little Russian along the way.

Through a series of events, I began to sense God's call to a new area—a country where it was illegal to become a follower of Christ. I knew that God was calling me, but it was so hard for me to change—to give up my visits with my Belarusian friends and branch out into a difficult place. But it was also exciting. I had been asked to come and secretly meet one of the most wanted men in this country—a church-planter and evangelist whom God was using to spark revival everywhere he went. He had never had any biblical training, and I was going to be his mentor. I arrived after almost twenty-four hours of travel and was immediately told by our undercover missionaries that it was too dangerous for him to meet me. The whole meeting was off.

Being the spiritual man I am, I immediately began to silently gripe at God. "Why did You bring me here anyway? I *could* be in Belarus, where I'd actually do some good."

I arrived at the hotel, exhausted and grumpy, and the first person I met was the hotel manager. I'll call him Chan. Chan surprised me by speaking perfect English. When I told him my name was John, he smiled and quietly said, "That's a Bible name, isn't it?"

Well, now my spiritual antennae were up, and I began to wonder who this man was. Later, missionaries told me that there were rumors that he was a believer, but that he might also be a government spy. They suggested that perhaps God had brought me there to find out which one. After several conversations with Chan, I decided to take a chance, and I told him I was an American pastor. I thought he was going to pass out. He ushered me into a private office and poured out his story. Not only was he a believer; he was the coordinator for training for *all* of the young pastors in half of the country! He would bring them into the hotel as cover and train them there. Chan said, "John, I have been praying for an American pastor who could come and help me. And here you are!"

I had come to train one man, and God gave me many—more than I could handle! Some of the young leaders in this underground church hadn't even been baptized yet. They didn't know who was supposed to do it. Do you know what it's like to baptize people in a hotel bathtub on the other side of the world? I do. And you never get over it!

This SIP was almost too much to drink! And it still hasn't ended. I went back the next year for more. And the year after that, God gave Chan a SIP of his own. He applied for a visa to come to America, which seemed unlikely. But the phone in my office rang one day and it was Chan calling me—from America. He couldn't believe it himself, but he was here—to study for the ministry and go back better equipped to serve and lead in a dangerous place. He won't be alone. When he goes back, I'll be going regularly to help him. Who would want to miss this?

One day, sitting in Chan's office at the hotel, a few of us sang Chan's favorite song. We sang it in a whisper so no one would hear:

Shine, Jesus, shine! Fill this land with the
    Father's glory.
Blaze, Spirit, blaze! Set our hearts on fire.

Flow, river, flow! Flood this nation with grace
  and mercy.
Send forth Your Word, Lord, and let there
  be light.

And let there be power, Lord! Resurrection power!
Welling up in us until it overflows. You don't have to stay
stuck in the past. And why would you want to? Aren't
you getting thirsty right now? Can't you just about taste
the next cool, refreshing SIP of God's power? *Pour it out,*
Lord! By faith, with the power of the past broken and the
future rich with your promise, we are ready to drink!

CHAPTER NINE

WINNING THE PRIZE OF AUTHENTIC POWER

*...and straining toward what is ahead, I press
on toward the goal to win the prize for which
God has called me heavenward in Christ Jesus.*

PHILIPPIANS 3:13–14

*Life's splendor forever lies in wait about
each one of us in all its fullness,
but veiled from view, deep down, invisible,
    far off.
It is there, though, not hostile, not reluctant,
    not deaf.
If you summon it by the right word,
    by its right name, it will come.*

FRANZ KAFKA, DIARIES

I t's shocking when you think about it. All that is
available to every Christ-follower and yet invisible
or ignored by so many. Maybe while reading this

book, you have been surprised to discover how *much* you have been missing. Well, there's good news on two counts. First, Kafka is right: Life's splendor is waiting to be found. The splendor of God's power is there for you in all its fullness, and we know the "right name." All power is in His name and comes through His name. And second, the past need not keep you from His power.

Every Christmas, New Hope, the church where I was pastor, presents a massive production that combines a passion play, an original drama, and a living Christmas tree. Thousands come and many lives are changed. It has been one of our best opportunities to reach new people.

My wife, Donna, and I always reserve a section for the friends we invite. Last Christmas, during the intermission, we went to greet people in the lobby. As my wife walked up the aisle of the worship center, she noticed every head turning to follow her, and she could hear people laughing. She had no idea what was going on until she came out into the foyer and someone semi-graciously pointed out the problem. She had sat on the sign from the pew in our section. And now attached to her rear end was a sign that read "Reserved for Pastor."

Paul could write that he was *straining toward what is ahead* because the power of his past was broken. He was now free to run the race to win. And we are too. A sign is stuck on all that is "behind" you that says "Reserved for Christ." It is not a weight to carry in the race any longer.

And so off we go—*ahead*. But what is ahead? There is so much we can't know, but this one thing—*we can know Christ. And the power of His resurrection*. This is the prize Paul was running after, straining toward with his very life. This is the prize worth everything, the pearl of great price, the splendor of life unrealized by most but waiting for you—*authentic power!*

DECIDING TO WIN

I don't understand people who don't desperately want to win. (Paul sure did: "I press on toward the goal to win the prize" [Philippians 3:14]. Maybe that's why I relate to him so well!) I've played competitive sports over the years—football, archery, racquetball, wrestling—but I only play individual sports now because I am so competitive that it's bad for my blood pressure! I just hate to lose. And I hate to see those I love lose. I have to be careful not to be one of those parents who gets thrown out of his kids' games. I don't get upset at my kids when they lose, just upset *for* them. Frankly, I think it bothers me more than it bothers them.

That's why I love God's authentic power. No one has to lose. The only way we can lose and miss God's power is if we run on the wrong track—our own! That's exactly what Paul was trying to avoid.

The Greek word for *goal* does not mean "finish line." It literally means "according to the marker." Paul was determined to press on and win according to the marker—in other words, by running on the right track. He was looking at the next step ahead of him to be sure that he wasn't running on his own, that he was taking that step *in the power Jesus had as He came out of the tomb.* Paul didn't want to find himself running outside the resurrection realm.

I want to win like Paul. And I want you to win. So let's look at the track that will take us there and use these markers to check our progress into authentic power.

MARKER #1: REMEMBER THAT HIS PROMISE IS ALREADY YOURS.

You don't have to *achieve* power, as our culture tricks us into believing. You *receive* it as His Spirit resides in you. Acts 1:8 tells us so clearly: "But you will receive power when the Holy Spirit comes on you; and you will be my witnesses in Jerusalem, and in all Judea and Samaria, and to the ends of the earth."

MARKER #2: GO AFTER GOD DESPERATELY.

Keep a close eye on your pursuit. We so easily veer off the track chasing lesser power. Pursue *God*. Regularly ask yourself if you are living in the power Jesus had as He came out of the tomb. Is the evidence for that power clear in your life? If not, correct your course. Abandon your pursuit of counterfeit power.

MARKER #3: EMBRACE STRATEGIC SUFFERING AND DEATH.

You are going to suffer. Everyone does. But few embrace it as a strategic tool of power. Suffering leads to death, but this is good news! As you die to your own power, you become an empty vessel for His. And death leads to resurrection—and to resurrection power in the here and now.

MARKER #4: PURSUE BIG POWER THROUGH SMALLNESS.

You can't own the power of God. You are not Him. But if you will be owned by Him, He will display His power through you. You have to decide whether to live in the power that lifts *you* up, which will never be real power at all, or live in the power that lifts *Him* up, which is authentic resurrection power. You will experience the greatest power where you are noticed the least.

MARKER #5: PURSUE YOUR PURPOSE IN LIFE AS A JOURNEY.

God's power is an adventure in progress. You don't arrive at a system or destination where you have somehow "achieved" power. You are on the journey of a lifetime, going deeper and deeper into His purpose and power. Look at your life to be sure you are on a balanced journey into the whole person God wants you to become.

MARKER #6: PASS THE TRANSITION TEST.

Go back to chapter 7, review the transition test, and use it to guide you through those few major transitions in your life where God is calling you, through change, into His greater power. You must turn the right way at these major transition points to stay on His track. Build lasting castles, not sand castles.

MARKER #7: BY FAITH, BREAK THE POWER OF THE PAST.

The past doesn't own you; Jesus does! Walk away from what has kept you from His power. You can. Pray the prayer for authentic power in chapter 8, and leave your powerless past behind.

MARKER #8: EXPECT SIPS OF RESURRECTION POWER.

Look for God's power all around you! Ask Him for those sacred, intimate places of power that will change you, embolden your faith, and fill you with His joy. Move boldly into your power filled future!

WHAT ABOUT IT? Are you on the right track? Running toward the right goal? What could be more important? Will you really be content to passively live your life and let the scenery pass by while you miss the heart of it all?

An American general once asked Winston Churchill to look over the draft of a speech he was going to make. Churchill told him the speech had too many passives. "What if I had said, instead of 'We shall fight on the beaches,' 'Hostilities will be engaged with our adversary on the coastal perimeter'?"[31]

Enough of wimpy Christian passivity! Let's charge the adversary in the power of the risen Christ! Let's go win! If that's what you want to do, then decide so.

Right now—decide to move from reading and absorbing these words to answering what Christ has called you to.

That's how we win.

RUNNING TO HIS VOICE

Just reading a book doesn't usually change my life. Reading my book probably won't change yours either.

Unless in the midst of it, God calls.

You see, that's how my life has been changed—through answering those clear calls of God. Paul was running to God's call—"to win the prize for which God has *called me heavenward* in Christ Jesus" (Philippians 3:14). I want to run there with him. God's call represents His promise to you because He never calls you to something He won't give you. God calls you to power—He has given you His power.

But it could be easy to misunderstand this call. He is not calling us to heaven—not yet. The NIV translates His call as *heavenward,* but the Greek word is simply *up.* In fact, this word is used nine times in the Bible and is never translated as *heaven,* nor are any of its related words. Paul literally refers to God's "up-calling."

This incredible section of God's Word finishes not with a call to heaven, but with a call to live with heaven's power *now.* In John 2:7 the word is translated "filled to the *brim,*" referring to the jars of water Jesus turned to wine. God is calling you to *all* of His power, to be filled to the brim with it, to live like all can, but few ever will, in the resurrection realm.

Do you hear Jesus' up-calling to you right now? It will change your life. It is a calling to be where Jesus is at every moment. As Paul says, it is *in Christ*. And where is He right now? Ephesians 1:21 uses the same word *up*, translated there as *above*. Christ is "far *above* all rule and authority, power and dominion, and every title that can be given, not only in the present age but also in the one to come."

Jesus is *up*—above all earthly power to hinder what God wants to do in you. He will be there forever, but He is also there now. And He calls you to be there with Him. To live in His authentic power, you must answer that call. You must run to His voice.

ANSWERING HIS UP-CALLING

If you are hearing His call, if you know that He is calling you up to His resurrection realm—to a different place than where you have been living—how do you answer Him?

WAKE UP WHERE YOU ARE

Most people think that answering God's call means going somewhere. Sometimes it does, but more often it means awakening to God's presence right where you are.

I tell a lot of stories, many about amazing experiences I've had. People often say something like, "I wish I could have those kinds of things happen to me! But my life just isn't like that."

I always want to shout, "But *my* life isn't like that either!" I'm not a celebrity or a world leader or a famous athlete. I'm just a preacher. But I really believe that I can live *His* life. And that He is going to exciting and powerful places. What bothers me is how much of His life and power I miss because of all the times I charge forward on my own. But my desire is to be fully awake to what He is doing all around me. That needs to be your desire too. It's the first step to answering His up-calling.

The first time I saw *The Passion of the Christ*, something stunning happened. As Jesus was being crucified and people all over the theater were weeping, I heard a strange noise beside me. I couldn't believe my eyes. The man next to me was sound asleep, snoring through the crucifixion!

The second time I saw the movie, I heard the same sound, this time behind me. A different guy, snoring away. His wife had to poke him to awaken him when Jesus rose! I still can't believe that anyone could sleep through that movie. I think God allowed me to see that as an example of the way many believers live. Asleep to the crucified, risen Christ who is on the move all around them.

I don't want to sleep! And I don't think you do either.

So wake up to where you are right now. Watch what happens today. Pay attention to who you meet. Look for something just a little out of the ordinary. That might be the first whisper of God's up-calling. Remember how Jesus said that if you want to be great, you must become a servant? What if you decided to serve those around you today in small ways? Do you think Christ's power might be unleashed in big ways?

Just the other day, I walked in to the Atlanta airport lugging three big bags. A woman named Wolina, who works for Delta, saw me and said, "Let me carry one of those." That had never happened before! As she carried my bag to the counter, I said, "I've never had anyone carry my bag like that before. That was really nice of you."

She patted me on the arm and said, "When God has been as good to me as He has, I just have to pass on His love to others!"

I was so impressed that I gave her a copy of my book *The Passion Promise*. She began to openly rejoice. Those around us looked on curiously. Another Delta employee said, "She's always like this. She is so kind to everyone that they always want to know why, and she shares her faith with them." What power!

But maybe you feel like your life is in a rut and even when you begin to awaken to God's work around you, you still don't like what you see. I was at the gym recently and saw something you don't see every day. A soldier was running at full speed on the treadmill—in full gear, strapped with a field backpack almost as big as him. I found out later that he was about to be deployed to Iraq. Just because you're running in place doesn't mean you're going nowhere. God may be preparing you right now for the next adventure that lies ahead.

Wake up where you are!

RISK POWERLESSNESS

Often the up-calling from God that will change your life can only be answered by your willingness to throw away the security blanket of your own power. We want to follow Jesus, but often we hedge our bets. We create a safety net just in case He doesn't come through. But if you really want His power, you have to trust His power.

If He calls you to do something that doesn't make sense financially, will you do it? If He calls you to do something that is not your personal preference, will you trust that His way is where real power lives? Do you ever allow yourself to reach the place where you are absolutely, completely dependent on Him? The great missionary Hudson Taylor once wrote to his wife, "I have twenty-five cents—and all the power of God." That's an exciting, powerful place to be.

Allow yourself to be there when God calls, without backup plans of your own.

EXPECT DARKNESS

God's up-calling is not to heaven yet. You can still expect plenty of battles in this life. In fact, it is often in the darkness that God's power shines brightest. Remember, the resurrection realm was birthed in a dark tomb.

I know full well that the darkness we face in this world can be overwhelming. I have seen it in the lives of so many I have served as pastor. I have faced it in my own life. Sometimes the dark opposition is so frightening and formidable that God's call sounds distant and faint. I sometimes feel a kinship with comedian Robert Orben, who once said, "Sometimes I get the feeling the whole world is against me, but deep down I know that's not true. Some of the smaller countries are neutral."

Surprisingly, this should be exciting news. C. S. Lewis

wrote, "Enemy occupied territory—that is what the world is. Christianity is the story of how the rightful King has landed, you might say landed in disguise, and is calling us all to take part in a great campaign of sabotage."[32] He's calling us! And who better to answer the call to walk through the darkness than those who are vessels of light? What we do in the darkness matters.

No event in my lifetime has brought such darkness to so many in America as Hurricane Katrina. I have just returned from a week on the devastated Gulf Coast. Thousands upon thousands were literally plunged into the darkness of floodwaters and utter destruction. I met God's people there. I expected to find despair. Instead I found power. I went as a part of my own denomination's relief efforts. As I write this, Southern Baptists are serving millions of meals, cleaning houses, cutting trees, saving lives, restoring hope, and sharing Jesus. I watched Pastor Rossi Francis of Grace Temple Baptist Church in Gulfport, Mississippi, lead his people to serve their community. His own church building was devastated but *the* Church was filled with power! I commented to him that he seemed almost happy. He said, "We are not disheartened at all. God has said to us, 'Move! I am going to let you be salt and light.' And we are moving. We have good news in the darkness. This is revival for us!" And perhaps it will be revival for all of us. The chance is there because God's power has always shone brightest in darkness.

Friends of ours from New Orleans, Preston and Diane Nix, and their two precious girls, Rachel and Rebecca, are living with us for a while. They lost everything they owned in Katrina. But they have not lost God's power. During this time I have had some of the most vulnerable and personal discussions with Preston that I have ever had with anyone. And I have seen Authentic Power in him and his family. They are willing to trust Him, and to suffer, so that they may know His power. I have seen it! I am watching it right now. His power is not theology to be studied. It is life to be lived. And His power dwarfs hurricanes.

In the darkest days for Martin Luther, his very life on the line in his battle for the truth of God's Word, he wrote, "And though this world with devils filled should threaten to undo us, we will not fear for God has willed His truth to triumph through us." We will not be undone! The darkness does not have power unless we surrender. God has willed that His truth triumph through you—even when His call leads you through darkness.

COME OUT OF HIDING, AND ANSWER HIS CALL

When it comes to God's power, we are still much like Adam and Eve in the Garden, hiding from God (Genesis 3:8). We are ashamed of the powerless lives we lead and afraid of changing. So we hide within our artificiality, content to be not any worse than other Christians we know, but in danger of becoming those "having a form of godliness but denying its power (2 Timothy 3:5).

And yet, as with Adam and Eve, the Lord's response to us is consistent: "But the LORD God called..." (Genesis 3:9). God will not easily leave us in our hiding places. He loves us too much. Far too many of His children have already lived out their lives devoid of the power that is meant to be theirs. And so He continues to call—maybe to you right now.

When my daughter Amy was five years old, we had a party at our house. Amy kept grabbing cookies off the table until they were about to run out. I told her not to eat any more. A little while later, I noticed that she had mysteriously disappeared. After a brief search, I saw a small pair of feet sticking out from behind a large potted plant in our den. Moving the plant aside, I discovered my daughter, covered in crumbs. "Amy," I said, "did you eat another cookie?" I had to stifle a laugh when she answered, "I think that maybe I probably did not!"

We really don't have to hide anymore. We can answer His call, covered in crumbs, with all our fears and failures. We can come powerless into power. That's the wonder of the Cross and the empty tomb. And it is worth the risk for you to answer His call.

I remember the first time I heard God's up-calling in my life—and answered His call. It changed me and ushered me into a life of His power. I was a teenager and a new follower of Christ, and I wanted to tell everyone how He had touched my life. One summer night I shared my testimony and sang at a small mountain church. Everyone left after the service, and my dad was a little late picking me up. I sat on the steps of the church alone, thinking.

Though I had decided to follow Jesus and would never turn back, it hadn't been easy. Many of my old friends no longer wanted to be friends. My best friend had just moved away. I was lonely. I began to wonder if I was the only person my age spending his summer Sunday night this way. I began to battle with the darkness.

Suddenly a strong wind blew through a wheat field next to the church. And the wind of God's Spirit began to speak to my soul. I opened the Bible that lay on my lap, and God began to call me—to call me *up*—to where He was and where He was going. I can't tell you exactly what happened that night. It's too personal, and I couldn't explain it if I tried. But I knew in that moment that if I continued to choose God's road, I would never lack for power and adventure. Thirty years later, I remember that experience like it was yesterday. And God has been true to His promise and to the many up-callings I have heard from Him since.

I feel sure that you are hearing His call too. Because as I wrote these words, I stopped and prayed that you would. That as you read this, something real would happen, that God would call you in His own way, personal to you, and life changing. I am praying right now that you will answer that call, and climb to the top of the victor's stand, where Jesus waits for you with the prize of His power, which He won for you and has been waiting so long to give you.

here is the power of the resurrection?"

Remember my friend Gary's question? I hope the answer is clear to you now. But I hope you do more than *find* authentic power. I hope you decide to *live* it!

Sadly, the Indian restaurant where Gary asked me that question has closed already. Not enough curry lovers, I guess. Almost everything around us is temporary, isn't it? All the more reason to live in a realm where everything is eternal, where our lives matter, where our next moment can be so filled with the power of God that history can be changed. That's the resurrection realm.

As I write these final words, I'm on a writing retreat at the beach. A storm is brewing outside. I'm watching the wildness of the water, the crashing of the mighty waves. And I'm drawn in awe to what God says about the waves of the sea: "For I am the LORD your God, who churns up the sea so that its waves roar—the LORD Almighty is his name" (Isaiah 51:15). I know that He is the Creator and Master of all this power: "He alone stretches out the heavens and treads on the waves of the sea" (Job 9:8). And that at any time He desires, He can still this or any other storm: "Even the wind and the waves obey Him" (Mark 4:41). And the amazing thing? More power than this is yours! *Resurrection power* is your design.

Just before I ended my pastorate at New Hope, I was talking to people after the service at the front of our worship center. A line had formed, and the first two people each needed several minutes of counsel. I noticed that standing third in line was a young boy around five or six years old. He waited quietly until it was his turn. I knelt down to look him in the eye. "You sure did wait patiently," I said. "Would you like to talk to me about something?"

He shook his head no.

"Are you sure?" I said. "You can talk to me about anything you'd like."

He shook his head again.

I knelt there, unsure of what to do next, when the little boy smiled slyly at me and smacked me on the arm.

"You're it!" he said and ran down the aisle.

Now, I'm too much of a child at heart to let him get away with it, so I chased him. I caught him at the door to the worship center, popped him on the back, and said, "You're it!" But this boy was fast! He caught me just as I reached the front again and slapped me right on the rear.

"You're it!" he said and took off.

The rest of the people in line to talk to me were now staring as if they weren't sure they needed my counsel after all. So I slapped the next guy in line on the arm and said, "You're it!" A senior lady next to him gave him a look as if to say, "No way, buster." He touched her on the shoulder and said, "You're it!" Looking unsure, she turned to the man next to her and quietly said, "Well, you're it."

And the game was on! A massive game of tag broke out in the worship center. It's the most fun I've had in church in a long time.

And as I reflected later, I felt that God smiled on that game. It was an illustration of His plan, His design for us. You really are *it*—His love, His plan, His design, His vessel for His life and power. If you look with spiritual eyes, you'll see it. Look at Jesus, coming out of the tomb, coming out in the power of His resurrection. And listen to Him as He tags you: "But you will receive *power* when the Holy Spirit comes on you; and you will be my witnesses" (Acts 1:8).

And now the world waits for your tag. Do you believe this now?

*You have the ability to live every moment in the same
strength Jesus had as He stepped out of the tomb.*

It's the *truth*. That's His authentic power for you. The
resurrection realm is here. That life of authentic power
begins now. But wait… In the howling of the wind and
the crashing of the waves, I think I hear something. Yes,
there it is. The whisper of God's voice.

*What, Lord? Yes, Lord, I hear You. I just can't believe
it. I am unworthy and amazed. How I love You, Lord! You
are awesome in Your power and love. Yes, Lord, I know this
message is not for me alone. I'll tell it to everyone I meet, from
Your heart to theirs:*

You're it!

NOTES

1. Elisabeth Elliot, *The Music of His Promises* (Ann Arbor, MI: Servant Publications, 2000), 54.
2. A. W. Tozer, *The Knowledge of the Holy* (San Francisco: HarperSanFrancisco, 1992), 2.
3. George Whitefield, "The Power of Christ's Resurrection," *Center for Reformed Theology and Apologetics*. http://www.reformed.org/documents/Whitefield/WITF_053. html (accessed 2 September 2005).
4. Tozer, *The Knowledge of the Holy*, viii.
5. *The Quotable ESPN*, ed. Shelley Youngblut (New York: Hyperion Books, 1998).
6. Toby McKeehan, Michael Tait, and Kevin Max, *Jesus Freaks, Volume 2* (Bloomington, MN: Bethany House Publishers, 2002), 28.
7. Paul Hattaway, *The Heavenly Man* (Derby, CT: Monarch Books, 2003).
8. As quoted on www.outreachofhope.org (accessed 20 October 2005).
9. John Henry Newman, "I Have My Mission," from *Meditations and Devotions* (1901), *The Feast of All Saints*. http://feastofsaints.com/newmanmission.htm (accessed 6 September 2005).
10. As quoted on www.gatewaytojoy.com (accessed 20 October 2005).
11. J. B. Phillips, *Your God Is Too Small* (New York: Touchstone, 1997, reprint), 109.
12. C. S. Lewis, *The Joyful Christian* (New York: Touchstone, 1997 reprint), 141.

13. Michael Scheuer, *Imperial Hubris: Why the West Is Losing the War on Terror* (Dulles, VA: Brassey's, 2004), 240.

14. Fyodor Dostoyevsky, *The Brothers Karamazov* (New York: Bantam Books, 1970), 127.

15. Robert Kurson, *Shadow Divers* (New York: Random House, 2004), 4.

16. A. W. Tozer, *The Pursuit of God* (Camp Hill, PA: Christian Publications, 1982).

17. C. S. Lewis, *The Screwtape Letters* (San Francisco: HarperSanFrancisco, 2001), 69.

18. Frederick Buechner, *The Hungering Dark* (New York: HarperSanFrancisco, 1985), 13.

19. Jim Collins, *Good to Great* (New York: Harper Collins, 2001), 28.

20. Ibid., 39.

21. Ibid.

22. A. W. Tozer, *Keys to the Deeper Life* (Grand Rapids, MI: Zondervan, 1988), 70.

23. Brian D. McClaren, *A Generous Orthodoxy* (Grand Rapids, MI: Zondervan, 2004), 191.

24. Richard J. Foster and James Bryan Smith, *Devotional Classics* (San Francisco: Harper, 1993), 107.

25. A. W. Tozer, *Best of Tozer, Book 1* (Camp Hills, PA: Christian Publications, 1978), 242.

26. From Chuck Swindoll, *The Tale of the Tardy Oxcart (And 1501 Other Stories)* (Nashville, TN: W Publishing Group, 1998), 163.

27. "Jim Elliot: The Seeking Life," *In Touch Ministries.* http://www.intouch.org/myintouch/mighty/portraits/ jim_elliot_213678.html (accessed 6 September 2005).

28. Michael L. Simpson, *Permission Evangelism* (Parisl, Ontario: Cook Communications Ministries, 2003).

29. "Wilberforce and Wesley," *bbc.co.uk Religion and Ethics.*
    http://www.bbc.co.uk/religion/religions/christianity/
    features/wilberforce/page6.shtml (accessed 6 September
    2005).

30. Elisabeth Elliot, *Music of His Promises,* 198.

31. Dominique Enright, *The Wicked Wit of Winston Churchill*
    (London: Michael O'Mara Books, 2001), 31.

32. C. S. Lewis, *Mere Christianity* (San Francisco:
    HarperSanFrancisco, 2001), 46.

Also from John Avant

When you settle for your own dreams, you're settling
for too little. These real-life stories will inspire you
to a life only God could imagine!

The Passion Promise
1-59052-311-3
US $11.99